Belongs to:
Father Angelo H. Camacho
O.P.
25 Loring St.
Som. Mass.

Leo the Thirteenth

THE FIRST MODERN POPE

Leo the Thirteenth

THE FIRST MODERN POPE

by Katherine Burton

DAVID McKAY COMPANY, INC.

New York

LEO THE THIRTEENTH:

THE FIRST MODERN POPE

COPYRIGHT © 1962 BY KATHERINE BURTON

First edition

NIHIL OBSTAT:

JAMES A. REYNOLDS, PH.D.
Censor Deputatus

IMPRIMATUR:

✠ FRANCIS CARDINAL SPELLMAN
Archbishop of New York

May 29, 1962

The nihil obstat and imprimatur are official declarations that a book or pamphlet is free of doctrinal or moral error. No implication is contained therein that those who have granted the nihil obstat and imprimatur agree with the contents, opinions or statements expressed.

LIBRARY OF CONGRESS CATALOG CARD NUMBER: 62-17443

MANUFACTURED IN THE UNITED STATES OF AMERICA

VAN REES PRESS   •   NEW YORK

Foreword

A DEFINITIVE life of Leo XIII is far beyond the scope of a single volume. Born Vincenzo Pecci in the Papal States when these were still possessions of the Church, as a young man, he was himself papal governor of several of them. He lived through the upheaval of 1860 and ten years later saw the total loss of all papal possessions save the Vatican alone. He became pope at a time when the papacy was, in the eyes of the world, a dying institution.

Leo never doubted. "If sometimes some hope the Church is on the point of death, she regains her rhythm always, that rhythm which crushed paganism," he said. In the course of his long life he lived through and was a part of losses and triumphs enough for half a dozen men. He was vitally interested in the problems that affected nearly every part of the globe—new governments replacing the old everywhere, ferment in the New World, rebirth and the accompanying revolutions in the Old, slavery in Africa. His encyclicals covered the joys and sorrows of the world, culminating in the magnificent letter dedicated to the cause of justice for the workingman.

Other popes have carried out coastal operations, as one writer has pointed out, but Leo was a man of the high seas. Justice to his life in a one-volume work can only be done if one selects. He was involved in so many large events that books on him tend to concern only his work and its effects on the world and the papacy. They do not tell enough of the story of the brilliant boy, the career man at the Vatican, the long years in Perugia in virtual exile because powerful cardinals distrusted his liberal ideas. They tend to neglect, though they tell at length of his encyclicals, the story of the man who thought he would die soon after he was elected to the papacy but who lived to complete twenty-five years of marvelous work.

All his life, even the last year, was crowded with work. When he lay dying at ninety-three years, he said to those about him, "I love you all but I am tired and glad to go." He had earned his rest.

He was like the great popes of other centuries, but he was also very modern. He set the standard for Catholic action so that it was no longer merely intellectual or political, but social and humanitarian, providing a share of life for all men. He did it because he loved justice for all people. He was a scholar, a poet, a diplomat, an able ruler, but his chief value was that he was great in both mind and heart. The old prophecy which gave him the title of *Lumen in Cælo* fitted him very well. He was indeed a light from Heaven shining on a tired world.

Leo the Thirteenth
THE FIRST MODERN POPE

Chapter One

WHEN, in the autumn of 1791, Count Ludovico Pecci brought his bride to his home in the ancient town of Carpineto, Italy, there was among their wedding presents one rather unusual one, a beautifully engraved card and on it a quatrain written by a poet friend of theirs:

> It may be of this union will be born
> A child beloved of God, a brilliant son,
> Whose glory shall in history extend
> Far as the sun his burning course doth run.

As poetry it was perhaps not of the highest quality; as prophecy it was excellent, for one of the sons born of that marriage was the child who would one day sit on the papal throne as Leo XIII.

He was born in March, 1810, the second youngest in a family of seven and was baptized in the family chapel Gioacchino Vincenzo Rafael Luigi. The second name was chosen by his mother who had a deep devotion to St. Vincent Ferrer.

Though Carpineto was not a far distance from Rome, it was far removed in its way of life. The town was very old and some said its name came from that of a certain Carpeto Silvio who had lived several centuries before the founding of Rome. The more prosaic but no doubt true account of the origin of the name was that it came from that of a tree very common in the area. In fact, a carving of such a tree had long been part of the coat of arms of the town.

In ancient days Carpineto had been occupied and partly destroyed by the Romans, and it suffered greatly from raids for hundreds of years afterward. The townsfolk, however, survived and became a brave and warlike band because of their experiences.

Members of the Templars had lived there. In the twelfth century Augustinian monks built a cloister. Later the Franciscans founded a monastery. In early days Carpineto had been for a time the feudal possession of the counts of Ceccano, a powerful family and bitter enemies of the papacy. In 1379 a battle was fought between the ducal family and the troops of Urban VI. It was then that the fortress town became a papal possession. In the days of the antipopes the town saw more strife but with the coming to the papal throne of Martin V the warfare came to an end.

During the sixteenth century Carpineto was in the hands of various noble houses, eventually becoming the property of the Borghese family whose coat of arms remains even in modern times on some of its old houses. By the close of the eighteenth century the town was completely in the possession of the Papal States until the loss of such properties in 1860. When Vincenzo Pecci was a boy, priests controlled the secular as well as the spiritual life of the people there.

One heard little in Carpineto of the stirrings of the great world outside. In fact, the town was so remote and so difficult of access that when Count Pecci took two of his sons to Viterbo, near Rome, to place them in school there, it took four days to make the journey.

There were many reasons for this isolation from the great world. Carpineto Romana—so called because it lay in the province of Rome—was built on a plateau and hung like an eagle's nest between two crags of the Volscian Mountains.

Ruined fortifications and broken walls showed that it had
been in more warlike days a difficult place to attack. In
the main it was no different from other ancient Italian mountain towns, all of them built on high rocks for fear of invaders. The invaders were gone long ago. Now the narrow
winding streets, with steps at intervals, and the miserable
lanes that passed for roads and made all travel difficult were
the principal dangers.

In the town of some five thousand people they were all,
save for gentry like the Peccis, farmers. Some had herds of
goats and cows; some worked for estates in the vicinity.
Since much of the land belonged to the Peccis, many small
areas were rented to the peasants on long leases. Each tenant
had his contract with the lord of the manor. The one exception was the vineyards which were each man's private possession. The mountain slopes abounded in chestnut trees
whose product was one of the chief industries of the area.
There were also orchards of fine fruit and olive trees.

The old castle where so many battles had been fought was
now the residence of the town officials. It had been rebuilt
and only one tower marked its earlier use as a fortress. The
home to which Ludovico Pecci brought his bride was, like
the rest, built on a high rock. It had been rebuilt often and
now most nearly resembled a French château. Its well-kept
sloping lawn and its tall trees were in green contrast to the
dark mountains behind and above.

In this house the children of Ludovico and Anna Pecci
were born. There they lived a life as different from that of
the world of Rome as could be imagined. When they climbed
to the roof of their house they could see in the distance the
hills of Sorrento and the great architectural mass that was
Rome.

When they walked the village streets, steep and winding,
they went past tall houses of gray stucco over brick. Small

black pigs darted across their paths and heavily laden don-
keys which were being driven to market clattered by. There
were no wagons—the streets were too narrow and far too
steep.

Often they stopped to say a prayer in the old Church of
St. Leo near their home or lingered at the town well where
the women came for water and a chat. They came home to
climb more steps, wide ones which led to the main door of
their house, with the family coat of arms above it. More steps
led to a great hall filled with heavy furniture and past that to
a picture gallery filled with the portraits of their forebears.
There were two modern ones hanging there, one their father
in the uniform of a colonel in the Italian Imperial Guard of
Napoleon; the emperor had been very proud of the military
skill of his foreign legion. The other was a portrait of their
mother, her hair powdered, in her right hand a fan, in her
left a plumed hat. On a table at one end of the room stood
the children's favorite ornament: a huge glass bell under
which was a collection of stuffed birds, brought long ago by
some ancestor from Austria.

The Pecci home was one in which the authority of the
father was supreme and the manners of a bygone age still
ruled. Count Pecci lived the life of his forebears, a patriar-
chal way where the past was more important than the present. He still wore the powdered wigs and the fine ruffled
shirts which most men had laid aside. He had no wish other
than to remain subject to the pope in the material world as
well as in the world of the spirit.

His wife called him always *Signore* and when the children
addressed their mother it was as *Signora mia Madre* and
their father as *Signoro mio Padre*. The formal address was
used by all. When the children came into a room where their
parents were they kissed their hands and made a bow. Yet,
despite all the formality and the old-fashioned manners,

there was a very deep affection among the members of the family.

Count Pecci was very busy with his various properties and with his leases. Countess Pecci devoted herself to her children to whom she gave her personal care. She was a very practical woman who taught her daughters to spin and sent her boys to help in the vineyards. Their father took his sons hunting, a sport to which every Pecci was devoted.

Anna Pecci often took the children with her on her errands of charity in the town. Carpineto had many poor people and help from the château was liberal. Countess Pecci was a very active Franciscan tertiary. The members of the Franciscan monastery had been dispersed by Napoleon and their property taken. When, after his fall, they came home again it was to utter poverty. The Peccis helped them to get back some of their property.

She was no mere Lady Bountiful. She went to the homes of the poor and sick; she fed and clothed them. In one year when the scant crops caused actual famine, she had bread baked for them in the château ovens, and great cauldrons of soup were always ready. She and her servants and her children brought medicine and food to the sick and needy. She was especially careful about aiding those who, normally able to help themselves, did not want it known that they must accept charity. To them she sent help secretly.

She worked to give the people some occupation besides farm work, her most successful attempt being the fostering of a silk industry in Carpineto by the introduction of silk-worm breeding there. This work, at first modest, eventually spread far beyond the town itself.

The Pecci children were taught to feel great pride in their ancestry. They knew the history of their mother's family.

The Prosperi-Buzi clan lived not far from Carpineto in a similar ancient stronghold. One of their ancestors was Cola di Rienzi, a civic leader of the fourteenth century who felt his mission was to end the rule of violence in Rome, to establish there a democracy and make Rome the peaceful capital of Italy, uniting the various dukedoms and kingdoms.

Vincenzo especially loved to hear stories about him, of his friendship with the writer Petrarch and various popes. Clement VI had given him great powers and he used them to crush the barons and to initiate reforms for the people. Later, under Innocent VI, he entered Rome in triumph, after having been involved in difficulties with reigning monarchs. An idealist always, he called himself "tribune of the sacred Roman republic" and tried to rouse a great interest in reforms for the populace. With the barons solidly allied against him, he met death in an uprising. Italy had never forgotten him and he was still a popular hero.

Old as was the bride's family, ancient too was that of the groom. In its long list were many distinguished names from the past. A Bishop Pecci had written a famous life of Saint Catherine. A Paoli Pecci had rewritten the statutes of Siena. One had often entertained under his roof Pope Martin V, and one had been ambassador under Charles IV. There were two blesseds in the family, one the founder of the Hermits of St. Jerome, the other Marguerite Pecci of the Servants of Mary. A cardinal at the court of Pius VII had borne the name of Pecci; another had been a well-known lawyer at that court. A Pecci had been a missionary in India and suffered martyrdom there.

Members of the Pecci family had been in Carpineto since Antonio Pecci came there from Siena in 1538. There he had come into conflict with the powerful Medicis so he fled the city with his family, thus establishing the Carpineto branch of the family. In the long gallery hung their portraits. The Pecci children knew them all.

Vincenzo Pecci was eight years old and his brother Giuseppe ten, when they were sent to a town close to Rome to begin their studies. Count Pecci was well aware that Carpineto was not the place to prepare his sons for the public life he hoped they would some day lead. He did not want to turn them over to antireligious influence either. When he heard that the pope had invited the exiled Jesuits to return and reopen their school in Viterbo, he made his plans to send them there. The boys were to make their home with their uncle Antonio, his brother, and study at the nearby academy.

The Eternal City had been through many difficulties in the years just past. Pius VII, a former Benedictine monk, had often declared when he was still a cardinal, that there must be a more democratic agreement between Church and state. In 1801 he made a concordat with Napoleon—a misplaced confidence, for the emperor was soon demanding concessions concerning religion which the pope found it impossible to grant. Seven years after the concordat had been signed Rome was occupied by French troops. Later Napoleon declared the Papal States annexed to France and in time made Pius VII a prisoner of state, exiling him to Fontainebleau. When the pope was able to return to Rome, Napoleon had become the prisoner. Rome was in a state of material and moral wreckage.

Even though the emperor had treated his prisoner with scant courtesy, the latter, after Napoleon's fall, gave haven to his family and asked the British to be gentler in their treatment of the fallen monarch. For a brief time Rome remained quiet in papal hands.

One of the pope's first actions when he returned from exile was to restore the Jesuits. This order had been dissolved

more than forty years before, by order of Clement XIV, and
at the demand of Spain and the Bourbon monarchs, as well
as some of his cardinals. However, Catherine the Great of
Russia and Frederick II of Prussia refused to publish the
brief of their suppression and the Jesuits had been able to
continue their work in those countries. Many people had
asked for their restoration in Italy and Pius VII recalled them
and invited them to reopen their schools.

Life at the academy was sheer delight to the boy from
isolated Carpineto. He was shy and delicate but he had also
been hardened by the simple and rigorous schedule in his
home and he fitted in well with the school routine. There had
been little opportunity for education at Carpineto. Now the
studious lad took great joy in delving into this new life of
the mind. He learned Latin so quickly that Don Garibaldi,
his teacher, told his colleagues that he was afraid to praise
the lad as much as he wanted to, because he did not want to
make him proud and overly assured.

It was fortunate that Vincenzo had made his early studies
with the Jesuits. For one thing, they put men of real learning as teachers even of the primary classes. They had taught
thousands of boys and young men the dogmas of their
Church, and had trained them to be defenders of the Faith.
However, they had taught also the humanities and the sciences. They understood, as did few teachers of the day, that
new ideas were entering the world and that they must be
met openly and not treated with disdain or ignored completely. Intellectual and material conditions were changing.
The boys they taught must be trained to meet them and, if
necessary, to change with them, keeping the old but adding
the new. Even if the new ideas had little or no value, the
boys, firmly guided in the ancient truths, could better cope

with the new ideas if they had been taught about them and knew what in them was wrong and what had value.

Then, too, the Jesuits had always taken a lively interest in the natural sciences, even though they were well aware that some felt such studies gave false interpretations of the Faith. They were excellent teachers for a transitional age for they taught their students the best from the world of the past and yet stressed what was good in the modern world. Though ultraconservatives feared their return, many others were happy to see them back, as was evidenced by the fact that hardly had they come back to their old school than the ranks of their classes were filled.

They felt a special pride when one of their students responded well to their teaching. So they were very proud of young Vincenzo Pecci whom they soon came to consider one of their most brilliant pupils. Even his literary style they praised to each other. One professor thought it was beginning to be very like that of Tacitus but another said that it was beginning to assume the impeccable form of Cicero.

Of such things Vincenzo of course knew nothing. He did know that he was very happy at Viterbo. He was not lonely for he had his brother Giuseppe with him and they lived at the home of their uncle. Then, too, there was no complete separation from the rest of the family. Occasionally the Peccis came to stay in Rome for a few months and during the vacations the two boys resumed their pleasant life in the town of their birth where they helped their mother with her charities and went hunting with their father. Summer was a delight but it was always equally delightful to return to the textbooks and the science laboratory at Viterbo.

Vincenzo was eleven years old when he wrote his first Latin verse, composed especially for his mother. She was so delighted with it that she sent him a basket of cakes and extra pocket money.

He was twelve when he wrote his second Latin poem, a quatrain in honor of a distinguished visitor to the school, Don Vincenzo Pavani, and in it he played on the fact that he and the visitor had the same given name:

> Your very name, Pavani, Vincenzo styled,
> Is also mine, who am a little child.
> The mighty virtues you so well pursue—
> Would I some day might win them too.

Chapter Two

WHEN Pius VII died in 1823, his successor was
Leo XII. Like Pius, the new pope had known exile. Like him
he had an awareness of a changing world. He dedicated himself to the cause of education, knowing that one could not
refute modern errors through ignorance of them. He greatly
increased the work of the Jesuits by placing them in charge
of many schools in the papal territory.

In 1825 he proclaimed a special jubilee year for the Christian world. It was a bold move, for many thought that only
a few would make the pilgrimage to Rome. However, people
did come, crowding the city, and the pope joined them
everywhere in the ceremonies and prayers.

Fifteen-year-old Vincenzo Pecci was deeply impressed by
the jubilee. With the other students he followed the pope
from church to church and at the final assembly at St. Peter's
he was one of thousands of young men who knelt in the
Belvedere Cortile of the Vatican while Leo XII blessed them
from a balcony.

Vincenzo had been chosen by the faculty to head a deputation of students and to give an address of thanksgiving to
the pope in Latin. Leo listened carefully and, when the
young man ended, gave him a special blessing. It was an
event that remained all Pecci's life a cherished memory.

In October of 1825 the Collegio Romano opened with
fourteen hundred students, among them Vincenzo Pecci. His

reputation for scholarship went with him to the new school. It was he who was chosen to deliver in the great hall of the college and before a full faculty and all the students, a Latin discourse which he had himself written, its subject: The Contrast between Pagan and Christian Rome.

In addition to languages his deep interest in the sciences was increasing. "In chemistry," he wrote joyfully home, "I observe the phenomena of nature. In astronomy I measure the distance of planets and the solar disk and admire the grandeur and majesty of their regular revolutions."

Suddenly all his youthful pride in his studies was shattered when word came to him and his brother that their mother was very ill. For the past two years she had not been well and in one letter Vincenzo had written her, "With the help of God and Our Lady I hope you will soon be better. To-morrow for your intention I shall make my Communion that your fever leaves you."

She was brought to Rome for medical treatment but there was no improvement. One day the boys were summoned in haste, Giuseppe, who had shortly before entered the Society of Jesus, and Vincenzo. They were her youngest, for the baby of the family had died some years before. She looked at them with deep love as they stood by her bed. She turned first to Giuseppe in his black suit and blessed him with her hand on his head. "My little cleric," she whispered, then turned to her younger son, kneeling by her bed, his eyes on her with a look of mingled love and fear. "Vincenzo, my second cleric," she said tenderly.

She was buried from the Church of the Forty Martyrs and in the brown habit of Saint Francis. On her tomb was carved, "Mother of the poor, of holiness and generosity."

A saddened Vincenzo returned to his school. Fortunately there was plenty of studying to be done and it helped allay his grief to work hard. That year he won the Latin poetry prize, after the successful completion of a very difficult assignment in which the competitors were given six hours to write a long poem, the subject announced only after they were seated in the lecture hall. That year he also won firsts in physics, chemistry and mathematics. The Jesuits considered him an excellent example of the student who would in future be the scholar.

"His work table was his world," wrote a fellow student of him years later. "It was paradise to him to be plunged in the study of science and his Latin verse and prose had a wonderful facility and excellence."

With his brother Giuseppe, the Jesuit scholastic, he studied the humanities and rhetoric for several years, following this with a three-year course in philosophy and the natural sciences. For recreation Vincenzo indulged in Latin versifying, changing to Italian now and then, and pouring out a variety of epigrams, hymns and odes, in hexameters and Sapphics and Ambrosian stanzas. During a serious illness, when he was twenty years old, he wrote an ode on what he was certain was his approaching end:

> Haggard and wan my face, laboring my breath;
> Weary I walk the way to dusty death.
> Now must I cheat my years of life who living crave,
> Since Atropos compels the dreadful grave.

At the end of the long poem he made it clear, however, that he was ready, for it ended:

> Happy the exile's feet to press the eternal land;
> Happy my storm-tossed ship will gain the strand.

His recovery was slow but complete and his verses became happier in tone. During that year he wrote in Italian a charming bit of light verse which clearly showed he was a part of the world around him:

Sylvia, of all the glory and the boast,
It was an English bard thy beauty sang
And gave to thee a future and a fame.

I too would offer now a gift—
This little rhyming flower,
Plucked from its grassy bower
Beside my garden's brook.

He was interested now not only in his studies but in the
world about him and his letters home often contained news
he thought might not have reached that isolated town. He
wrote sadly of France, a land he had already learned to love;
the king had dissolved the chamber of deputies and suppressed the freedom of the press. There had been fighting:
"the number of deaths and the wounded is in the thousands."
He wrote of events in Rome too—the death of Leo XII,
the election of Pius VIII and of his death not much over a
year later, the election of Gregory XVI, a scholar so erudite
that, wrote Vincenzo, "I have learned that Cardinal Wiseman of England, himself a great scholar, has spoken in high
terms of his [scholarship]."
His brother Giuseppe was very certain of his future, but
Vincenzo had not made up his mind. He was greatly lured
by the life of the dedicated scholar but he was also an ambitious young man who thought that a secular position at the
papal court might be excellent as a future. In this his father
encouraged him, anxious to have his brilliant son distinguish
himself in the world and feeling he could best do this by
service at the Vatican. But he was very proud of the young
scholar and gladly answered his request for a copy of the
works of St. Thomas Aquinas from the family library, ". . . at
once if I may have it. I need it very much. I am told that he
is the archimandrite of theologians." Another letter went to
one of his older brothers, also at Carpineto, asking him to

send "the gunlock I used last fall. I want to have it cleaned here." He added that he was buying powder for next summer's hunting.

On the other hand, though he was aiming for a secular career, he had not forgotten his mother's hope for him—her "second cleric." He began in 1830 at the Collegio Romano the study of theology as well as civil and canon law, as was the fashion among many young wellborn Romans of the day. At the end of his years of theology he was given an examination—to explain three treatises, on indulgences, on the sacrament of Holy Orders and on final unction. Three professors, known as Objectors, were to oppose his arguments. This was to take place in the great hall of the college, filled with cardinals, prelates and professors from the various Roman colleges.

Evidently he carried out the test well for the Diary of the college said it was very proud of him: "The young man showed such ability that great things seem to be in store for him."

When he received his doctorate in theology, he had still not made up his mind about his future but, urged on by Cardinal Sala, a man of considerable importance at the papal court, he asked to enter the Academy of Noble Ecclesiastics as another step to a possible future at the Vatican. To his utter amazement he was at first refused entrance. Doubt had been expressed in some quarters as to his eligibility. He must prove his ancestry was noble before he could be accepted.

His pride stung to the quick, the young man wrote a brief history of his family, beginning with the Peccis of Siena whose history was well documented. Then he produced later documents to show that his own family was a branch of the Peccis of Siena. He proved that his family had been forced to leave Siena centuries before due to political difficulties but showed the line had continued through the years. The evidence was clear and young Pecci was admitted. For five years he remained there, taking advanced studies in civil and canon law and receiving more degrees.

Even yet he was not certain that he wanted to become a priest. "Good reasons and good prospects offer themselves," he wrote to his brother Giuseppe. "With your sound judgment and desire to increase the glory of our family, you will approve whatever be my intention." He added that he had joined a literary society which he knew would aid his career. He hoped, if he did decide to become a priest, that he would rise in the Church and that his family would then be held in even greater esteem. For this he must seek patrons in high places so that he might rise "quickly and assuredly."

Cardinal Sala now, and for some years past, governor of the college, again took a hand in planning his protégé's future. Young Pecci was still in minor orders but the young man's record had been so excellent that popes and cardinals had been made aware of him. When his education at the college began, Leo XII was still living. When Leo died in 1829 a storm gathered regarding his successor. Leo XII had spent his brief reign in bringing to Rome the best educational facilities, feeling that, as the center of Catholicism, it ought to have them. He had restored a measure of order among the congregations, disorganized by Napoleon's actions against them. He had also decided that more advanced students should finish their studies in Rome and so had returned to the Jesuits the Collegio Romano which had formerly belonged to them.

For his successor the French and Austrian authorities had wanted a mild and unargumentative man, though others hoped for a man of firmness and decision. The conclave which chose him lasted five weeks but at last the cardinals agreed on a man. He took the name of Pius VIII but lived for a brief time only. He was pope from March of 1829 to December of 1830. Though he was a mild man, he was also one with a mind of his own. During the years when Rome was under French rule he had been arrested for refusing to take the oath of allegiance and had been for several years a prisoner. Soon after his election the English Catholic Emancipation bill was passed. It had been the great hope of Leo XII, who died before it was ratified.

Short as was Pius' reign it had its share of troubles. In July of 1830 came the revolution of that year in France. When he was dying word came of another revolution, this one breaking out in the Papal States. That, however, was a matter which the next pope would have to meet.

Gregory XVI had been a member of the Camaldolese, one of the most contemplative of congregations, and he had been forced into office against his will. He tried to combat the ever-rising forces of nationalism and liberalism. It was not that he was himself a reactionary; rather he was at heart a reformer. He knew, as did those who gave real thought to the future, that many of the old ideas and concepts were going and that the French Revolution had changed the old alliances between popes and kings and they would not return. He realized that one pressing question must be faced, the Church must decide to ally herself with the people against the state in an endeavor to make all people free, or that the papacy would strive to keep its spiritual supremacy and spread this power internationally.

In his second year on the papal throne he condemned the French priest Lamennais, who for some years fought, and very brilliantly, for free speech and a free press, neither of which he believed was possible under a royal government. With his friends Lacordaire and Montalembert he had founded a journal called *Avenir*, a good title for it was concerned only with the future. He was very much embroiled with conservative elements among the clergy in his own country, and eventually he came to Rome to plead his cause, only to find that Gregory had been turned against him.

Shortly afterward an encyclical, *Mirari vos,* came out condemning him and his work. Lamennais retired and soon after he left the Church. The incident marked the beginning of deep bitterness among members of the Church, conservatives and liberals both.

Young Pecci continued with his studies at the Academy of Noble Ecclesiastics, remaining there until 1837. By that time he had been well trained in a school whose chief aim was to educate future nuncios and specialists in various branches of Vatican administration and diplomatic office. He had during those years suffered from a severe illness and had been most annoyed about it. "These attacks interfere with my studies which are my sole concern," he wrote home, and spent his time recuperating in writing verses which both defied death and resigned himself to God's will.

Over the years various prelates had taken note of him, in part because of Cardinal Sala's promoting him in every possible way. It was he who suggested that the pope appoint young Pecci, still in minor orders, domestic prelate in the papal household. Later, as referendary, his duties were to read and answer petitions to the Holy See. When young Pecci heard of his new appointment, his first expressed thought was, "How this will please my father. He is very ill and he will be cheered by the news."

In November he was made deacon in the Chapel of St. Stanislaus in the Church of St. Andrew. And now, his studies completed, he went to live again with his uncle Antonio in the palace close to the Ara Coeli. He had a new office now, secretary to Cardinal Sala. When the latter suggested he go on to ordination, Pecci asked if he might wait a little longer before making his decision and the cardinal agreed.

He had hardly taken up his new work when a fearful epidemic of cholera broke out in Rome. Cardinal Sala was overseer of all the hospitals of the city and young Pecci became his devoted helper. Though not yet ordained, he could be of assistance in many practical ways. He could see that medical aid was given the sick and that comfort went to the mourning relatives during the days of terror and death. The young cleric went tirelessly from home to home, greatly easing the cardinal's heavy tasks. Pecci witnessed suffering and death and, much disturbed, he wrote his will. His brothers were to have anything he left after Masses for himself and twenty crowns for the poor of Carpineto and "to my Uncle Antonio the porcelain service presented to me by Cardinal Sala."

Not long after the plague was ended Cardinal Sala spoke again, and this time plainly, to his protégé—he must become a priest immediately. "You asked me to wait a little and it is now well over a year," he said. "If all the Roman aristocracy were as undecided as you the Holy Father might as well shut up the Nobles' College."

The cardinal had also hinted that the young man might soon be promoted to a post where his ordination would be necessary. Although Pecci was still thinking to some extent in terms of a career in diplomacy, he yielded to his patron and friend. Then, too, the brief experience of caring for victims of the plague and the fearful mortality in that plague had made him wish he could have given priestly services to the dying, for sometimes there was no time to call anyone.

On the last day of December, 1837, he was ordained by Cardinal Odescalchi. Many relatives and friends attended. His father had been ill for some time and he had feared he could not be present, but he was able to come and watch the ceremony in the front pew. The ordinand's server was his brother Giuseppe.

Count Pecci had been none too happy about the ceremony that made his son a priest. "Giuseppe is a Jesuit and I am resigned to that, but I cannot reconcile myself to the idea that Vincenzo may come back to us a village padre," he told his brother Antonio.

Though young Pecci had hesitated so long about the final step, now that he was a priest, he found himself very happy, so much so that for the first time in his life he felt a deep desire to leave the world entirely and give himself up to a life of contemplation. He had no wish to enter a religious order; had he felt that vocation he would have gone to the Jesuits. What he did feel, and strongly, was a desire to subordinate from now on every action to his career as a priest. He knew now that one could serve the Church as a secular priest, too, but he prayed that his spirit would not be dissipated in worldly matters.

Cardinal Lambruschini, the papal secretary of state, had, as soon as Pecci was ordained, given him further duties at the Vatican, which showed that the young man was being looked on as one of promise for the Church. Don Pecci was prepared and very ready to remain in Rome. However, he had been trained for administrative work and such men were needed in important places in the Papal States. It was very reasonable that, soon after Cardinal Sala had suggested, "Why not send him to Benevento?" the secretary of state decided this would be an excellent appointment.

In February of 1838 the pope appointed Don Pecci papal governor—which at that time and in that place meant civil governor—to Benevento. "Go there as soon as possible," he was told. "There is need that order be restored quickly."

"This is a very delicate mission," Cardinal Sala warned him. "You will have to deal with many people of varying opinions and with opposing parties. Be wary and judicious, but don't be entirely silent either, for then you would lose with both sides—but weigh your words."

It had been made very clear that the pope wanted a young and enthusiastic man for Benevento but apparently little thought had been given to the fact that the appointee was only twenty-seven years old and had, until that time, held no position of responsibility or authority, or that his Benevento assignment very evidently would mean the administering of a province. However, it did not trouble Monsignor Pecci either—he had been named to that honor earlier—and he was young enough to feel very pleased at being given a position which would offer excitement, responsibility and a new milieu.

His first letter to Cardinal Sala, after he reached his post, spoke of the "sluggishness, almost inaction" of some of the Catholics there and the "truly extraordinary activity of the Liberals." His first letter to Carpineto was full of news about the new work. He announced with evident delight that the sentries presented arms to him as if he were really a state official, the head of them all in Benevento—a thing which, it was evident from the letter, he could still scarcely believe was true.

Chapter Three

THE papal dependency of Benevento was some forty-six miles in area and was situated within the boundaries of the kingdom of Naples, not far from the capital. It had been almost continually under papal rule since the eleventh century but it was much more ancient than that. It still held the remains of a Roman theater and an arch of Trajan. Under the Romans the city had been an important commercial center on the Appian Way. It had an eighth-century church and a twelfth-century cloister.

Talleyrand had received it as a gift from Napoleon in more recent days and had called himself Prince of Benevento. But the title and the French rule had not lasted long and when the pope returned to Rome, Benevento came again into the possession of the Holy See. The Bourbon kings of Naples had been for years trying, but unsuccessfully, to buy it from the popes.

This was a very different town from Carpineto, also a papal possession. It was, like Carpineto, the home chiefly of peasants and farmers, but in addition it had a number of bankrupt barons and shabby nobles who used their palaces as if they were feudal fortresses. From there they defied law and public authority other than their own. Besides, because of its remote position, Benevento had become a favorite refuge of Neapolitan political refugees and even criminals

who took shelter there from the police of other cities. There were also roving guerrilla bands and a group of smugglers. To some extent the Benevento barons sheltered these from the law and were well repaid for their efforts. And it was to this lawless place that the young priest, still fresh from the schools, had been sent.

These lawbreakers were a minority, of course, but unfortunately they were the ones with power. There were many at Benevento who wanted only to obey the rightful laws and live in peace, but it was difficult. The taxes were very heavy, the pretext being that they were necessary to give the people protection. Petitions had been several times sent to Rome but the nobles had countered by saying that the people were lazy and loved to mix in politics of which they understood nothing. In addition, it was a papal refuge set up in the heart of a foreign government which added to the difficulty of controlling it. Several envoys sent there had given up their post.

Now word came to Benevento that a new delegate was coming from Rome, a young and untried man. The criminal element breathed more easily. This one would not be difficult to manage.

The young monsignor from the Vatican arrived, pleasant and very evidently ready to please. He was amazed to find people living in the palace which was to be his official home and even more amazed to learn they had no intention of leaving. These were not criminals, however, but highly placed officials, one of them the president of the courts, Signor Palomba, who had some time before been given a portion of the palace by Pecci's predecessor. He was obviously remaining with the intention of watching carefully every movement of the newcomer. Even Cardinal Sala, when Monsignor Pecci consulted him by letter, could not get rid of him or help either in evicting the Young Italy adherents who were also living there and working very openly with the radical elements in Naples.

Monsignor Pecci relieved his feelings, as he often did, by writing a little verse:

> From the Adriatic shore
> A dove—its brood to rear—
> Builds a fine nest above our door.

The meat in the brief verse was that Palomba was the Italian word for wild dove.

The new delegate had to some degree been informed as to what he would find in his new charge but, he now realized, far from fully. At first he avoided the barons and spent much of his time with the ordinary people, visiting them in their homes and talking over their problems with them. To this young, sympathetic man, evidently to be trusted and really interested in their troubles, they were soon pouring out their stories, their complaints about the harsh taxes and the wrong done them. Before long he had a much clearer picture of the situation at Benevento.

After some months he began visiting the barons and discussed with them the townspeople's grievances. They neither denied them nor argued them away. "I am afraid," he wrote to Cardinal Sala, "that the aim of some here is to seize the goods of others." He wrote of "factions and forbidden associations" which were rife there. He commented that the very men who should have worked most strongly for lawful government were not doing so, were, in fact, eager to bring about a change from papal rule.

Before he had left for Benevento Rome had made it clear that he was himself to handle matters which came up and so he neither asked for nor received help. For one thing, Rome was anxious to avoid conflict so that Naples could not put in a claim to Benevento. On the other hand, Monsignor Pecci

was well aware that the real power was his. He had pontifical soldiers under him. And he was utterly unafraid and
knew that, even if he had no direct help from Rome, he
would have no interference either.

Before long word spread that this young Pecci was very
alert and not easily fooled. Worst of all, he was honest. Now
he was beginning to have his papal soldiers arrest bandits.
There was fear he might next go after the barons who were
supporting them. A chill spread through the element that
saw its easy living endangered. Before long a request for his
impeachment went to Rome, a carefully worded document:
"Undermining of legitimate authority to the lords ... siding
with the peasants and inciting them to disrespect for su-
periors ... really an all but revolutionary ruler ... unwilling
to listen to friends of good government who have a stake in
the country"—these were the charges in the letter, and it
ended with the dark threat, "If he remains the Patrimony of
Peter will lose Benevento forever."

In Rome many who had known the young envoy since his
school days spoke up for him. "He has a deeply reflective
mind and I know he will never take a false step," said one
high official, and this reflected the opinion of many. Pope
Gregory, too, had more faith in his young minister than in
the injured barons. He refused to recall him and instead
gave him a free hand in his work. "You are granted all facul-
ties to assert your rights," wrote Lambruschini.

Fortified by high authority, Monsignor Pecci announced
an end of brigandage in Benevento on the ground that it was
illegal and criminal. The lesser men capitulated but the barons did not. Brigands were still paying them blackmail for
protection and the down-at-the-heels barons needed the
money. Then, too, some of the brigands, being openhanded
when they had money, were looked on as a variety of Robin

Hood by some, and this made it more difficult to apprehend them.

One day an angry baron stormed into Monsignor Pecci's office, insolently refusing to pay any taxes. He said he was announcing his refusal in person, adding that he was so powerful that he could have Pecci recalled in a week. "Anyway the law does not apply in my territory," he said, "and you have made arrests in my domain." The latter statement was true. Papal troops had entered and arrested a group of brigands sheltered in the baron's castle and jailed them in cells in the envoy's own palace.

Monsignor Pecci looked at him with interest. "Can any man be outside the law?" he asked.

The baron did not answer directly. "I'll go to Rome," he threatened, "and get the pope to give me an order to dismiss you from Benevento."

"Go by all means," said Monsignor Pecci courteously, "but do remember that before you make your complaint at the Vatican you must pass Castel Sant' Angelo." This was a real threat, for the angry baron knew well that Castel Sant' Angelo was a prison for political offenders.

Eventually the young envoy enlisted the co-operation of the Naples police against the lawbreakers. On collected evidence he had another castle entered by his troops and the fifteen brigands discovered there were arrested. Others who had been driven from Naples or run away from the police were returned. The people of Benevento were delighted at this swift justice. They were even more delighted when their governor adjusted the taxes more fairly and with some of the money began to improve the very poor roads, which meant opening markets for crops and industrial products. Monsignor Pecci had gone to Rome to ask Gregory if he might do this and was given permission. With new law and order in the city, Benevento's farms began to flourish. Farmers not only found new markets for their crops but could actually save money. Best of all, they could go about freely and not fear violence and terror through extortion.

He was not so successful in curbing the secret societies such as the Camorra, chiefly because it was difficult to find the members. People were unwilling to give evidence, fearing reprisals. However, his chief reward in his very difficult assignment was the love the people gave him. Once when he fell very ill, the whole town marched to the Church of Our Lady of Grace to offer prayers for his recovery.

At one time Cardinal Lambruschini consulted him regarding an offer from the King of Naples—the exchange of Benevento for a similar area nearer Rome. Monsignor Pecci urged that it not be done, that Benevento was valuable for the papacy. Negotiations were broken off. The reason he had given was not so much political as it was moral. The people of the city, freed now from unfair taxes and with industry developing, were much better off under the protection of the Holy See—why change?

After more than two years at Benevento, Monsignor Pecci was called back to Rome and given another assignment. King Ferdinand of Naples in a farewell letter congratulated him because, despite his youth and inexperience, he had been successful in a task which might well have taxed a veteran in the diplomatic service.

He came back to Rome in May of 1841 to find he was to be sent as delegate to Spoleto, an ancient Umbrian town which had been in papal hands since the thirteenth century. He was preparing to go there when the plans were suddenly changed and he was instead named papal governor of Perugia, the capital of Umbria. He was told there had been much revolutionary activity in Perugia and also great oppression of the common people, just as in the post he had left. Also, as had been the case at Benevento, there was considerable mismanagement and discontent.

Perugia had once been a powerful city of the Etruscans, later a medieval republic and was now a possession of the Papal States. Its ancient walls bore witness to its antiquity. Its university had been built in the fifteenth century. High on a hill above the wide green Umbrian plains, it was still called Perugia Turrena—the tower-girt city—because of the towers which had once been its chief defense.

In earlier years it had been famed for its great workers' guilds which had made the city rich. By 1841 it was entirely in the hands of the local aristocracy. The secret societies were busy among the people, especially the socialist groups. Perugia had in its midst a force armed to destroy the religious faith of the city.

Monsignor Pecci was given a fine reception at Perugia, even by the opposition. He soon found that the pattern of Benevento was to some extent repeated here, as he had been warned, but now he found cheaters rather than oppressors. At one time he learned that the bakers were selling greatly underweight loaves to their customers and, though many of these customers were very poor, they dared not object. Monsignor Pecci waited until he had investigated thoroughly. Then, assured that the facts were accurate, he one day suddenly ordered every loaf baked that day to be confiscated from the ovens and shops and given to the people for nothing. Examination on later days showed the size of the loaves to be normal and of honest weight.

The people in Perugia who had small modest properties were very much at the mercy of moneylenders. He called some of the latter to the palace to ask about their rates of interest. After long questioning and reluctant answers, and much evidence given by those in debt, he realized the moneylenders were asking interest so high that sometimes they received back three times as much as they had originally advanced.

"Then you are not moneylenders but usurers," he told them, "and that is a criminal offense. Pay back half of what you have extorted. There will still remain a good profit for you."

The returned money—for it was returned though with extreme reluctance—Pecci gave to the peasants to restock their farms and thus do away with much of the necessity for making loans at all.

Monsignor Pecci had been at Perugia only a brief time when word came that Pope Gregory had decided to make a visitation of the states belonging to the Church and Perugia was to be included in the itinerary. It would seem a simple matter to entertain him fittingly but it was not so simple. The city was built on an elevated plain and the road leading to it was all but impassable. Monsignor Pecci had a month to get ready and he used several weeks to build a new and good road, to the delight of the people, who were pleased to be honored with a visit from the pontiff but who were even happier to know that now they would have a fine new road in the future. It had already been named: Strada Gregoriana.

The rest of the month was devoted to getting ready to entertain the important visitor. When Gregory arrived the city was gaily decorated in his honor. He admired the fine road over which his carriage was driven but he was not told that it had been built just for him. It was evident that he enjoyed his brief stay, for when he was departing and had left with his host gifts for the people who had entertained him, he said, "Later, Monsignor, when I am back in Rome I shall remember you, too."

As he was leaving he halted his carriage briefly to speak

once more to his envoy: "Monsignor, in my travels I have
been in some places received like a monk, sometimes with
the ceremony due a cardinal—but never before a reception
which truly becomes a sovereign."

It had been a fine visit for the pope but the careful Pecci
had managed even in those few days to speak about reforms
he wished to carry out and had secured permission to pro-
ceed with them. Though in the city of Perugia he did not
have to get rid of brigands, there was plenty to do to improve the condition of the people and on this he could con-
centrate with little opposition.

He opened a savings bank, himself furnishing the capital
to open it. He spurred education, giving the long neglected
Collegio at Spello a new curriculum and new professors. It
became so good that the best families in Umbria began to
send their sons there. He reorganized the municipal government and the courts of justice, ending interminable delays in
court proceedings by bringing everything under one roof.

All the reforms were good but undoubtedly his chief
monument was the savings bank where farmers and small
tradesmen could keep their money safely. And, by getting
loans there, and at low interest, they could keep themselves
out of the clutches of usurers.

Both at Benevento and at Perugia the future pattern of
Pecci's thinking and his life itself were already developing,
as was his keen interest in the problems of the working people. It was a real interest for he went among them and talked
with them, a rare thing for an official of that day to do. He
listened to their troubles and when possible helped correct
the wrongs under which they suffered. It was during those
early years that he learned to understand how workingmen
lived and also how to cope with antagonistic statesmen. He

saw why education was so weakened—at first it had been by
the many and long wars, and now it was by revolutionary
Jacobinism and the secret societies. That was why so much of
his time was given to establishing new schools and to reforming old colleges. One other thing was certain about
Monsignor Pecci—the old indecision about his work was
gone. Cardinal Sala would have no complaints to make about
that now.

When Gregory left for Rome after his visit to Perugia, he
had said that he would remember Pecci when he was at
home again. Early in 1843 the promised gift came. Monsignor Pecci was recalled to Rome, this time to be sent as
nuncio to Brussels to replace Monsignor Fornari who had
been appointed to the post in Paris.

For this new appointment it was necessary that Pecci have
a higher title. Therefore, on January 27 Pope Gregory named
him archbishop and gave him the titular Church of San
Damiata in Rome. He was consecrated by Cardinal Lambruschini at San Lorenzo.

As he had done with earlier honors, he sent all the documents pertaining to his consecration as archbishop, as well
as those on his new and very important appointment, home
to Carpineto. This time he added one thing more—a portrait
of himself in his new robes of office. "Hang it between the
portraits of our parents," he wrote.

He left Rome for Brussels as soon as possible for he wanted
to see the departing nuncio and get from him suggestions
about the work ahead. It was a task that daunted him, but
perhaps he would have been even more daunted had he
known with what misgivings the former nuncio viewed the
appointment of this comparatively unseasoned young man
to the difficult and complicated nunciature in Belgium.

Chapter Four

THE assignment to Brussels was a very different one from the young diplomat's first two. In both of those his had been the governing power, for Benevento and Perugia were possessions of the Holy See. In Belgium he would be merely the representative of the pope. A king headed the Belgian government, but, as in any limited monarchy, the people were sovereign. Belgium had a constitution and a parliament made up of members the people had chosen themselves.

In Rome Archbishop Pecci had been carefully briefed by Cardinal Lambruschini, who explained to him that the new state constitution of Belgium gave freedom of religion. The state could not, however, appoint ministers from other lands.

The cardinal had also told him that the previous nuncio had opened a Catholic university there. He said word had recently come to the Vatican that some of its professors were greatly under the influence of the doctrines of Lamennais, whose book, *Paroles d'un Croyant*, was being read widely though the author was now not only out of the Church but styled himself an unbeliever.

"In many ways you will find it a difficult mission," the cardinal warned the new archbishop. "You will have to be careful not to come out with too many opinions—and yet," he added with a wry smile, "you cannot always remain silent either." The prelates were an excellent group of men, he said—"in the main"—and Pecci must be extremely careful to consult with them whenever possible.

As for the political situation, this Archbishop Pecci knew was very complicated. In 1815 Belgium and Holland had been united by the Congress of Vienna to form the kingdom of the Netherlands, but the union had not worked out well. The Belgians had fewer representatives in the assembly than Holland, yet there were more Belgians than Dutch in the population. Fifteen years after it was formed the union was legally dissolved—by that time it had all but broken apart. The Belgians eventually formed a separate state, their neutrality guaranteed by France and England. It was at the time the youngest kingdom in Europe, not more than a dozen years old. Prince Leopold of Saxe-Coburg-Gotha, a Protestant, had been chosen its first king. His queen, Louise, was a daughter of Louis Philippe and a Catholic.

The state was Flemish in character. It was in every way very different from the Papal States. In addition there was continual argument and dissension between religious and secular authorities. The Liberal party and the Church party battled without ceasing on the matter of education.

One handicap for the new nuncio was that he knew very little French. All the way to Brussels he studied that language. When illness delayed him for several weeks at Nîmes, he used the time for further study. When he reached Brussels, though his accent was still poor, he could at least make himself understood.

King Leopold received him at his first audience. Archbishop Pecci found the monarch a pleasant, friendly man who made him very welcome and assured him that, though he was not himself a Catholic, he saw to it that Catholic interests were respected.

"I hope Your Majesty will be indulgent," the new nuncio said. "This mission is entrusted to me by the Holy Father and so I must speak always in the name of Belgian Catholics." Both knew exactly what the other meant—there had been argument about the number of Catholics elected to the parliament—but neither was more explicit about it.

"For thirteen years, Monseigneur," said the king, in a somewhat oblique reply, "it has been my aim to have good Catholic deputies here. They have always been on the side of law and order and tranquillity for my state and I do my best to be fair with them." Soon afterward, as if in confirmation of his good intentions, he came with the entire royal family to the parish church of La Chapelle for the ceremonies of the Coronation of Our Lady.

It did not take long for the nuncio to realize how delicate a mission he had been given. For one thing, anti-Christian groups were fomenting trouble. And here Pecci had no papal troops to call on if trouble came. The matter of education was a cause of great argument with the Liberals and the Church engaged in continuous strife, the Church insisting on her right to teach Catholic children in Catholic schools, the Liberals insisting that all education be nondenominational. There was no real interference but there was continuous nagging by the latter groups, and, as the cardinal had said to Pecci, one could not always be silent.

The years in Brussels were to be packed with argument and opposition, but much of it came from his own coreligionists. He was able to bring about some reforms and he made many friends, but at this post he did not see much of the people in the lower walks of life. His days were spent with high ecclesiastics, all older than he and much more experienced, some of them openly critical of him from the beginning. Hitherto he had had assignments where he gave the orders. Here tact was needed even to make suggestions.

He had not realized that almost from the month of his arrival there had been complaints about him sent to Rome. Prince Metternich, the Austrian chancellor, whose country retained a keen interest in the former Hapsburg province of Flanders, wrote to the papal secretary of state that this young man seemed unable to keep the peace by restraining the high clergy as the previous nuncio had done so skillfully. "He seems to be unwilling to exercise this moderating influence," he wrote darkly, and added that he was a good lad, but with little initiative or knowledge of the world. Later he might be worth-while diplomatic material, but hardly now and certainly not in Belgium.

Then, too, the diplomat whom he had replaced was continually sending messages from Paris to him suggesting that Pecci ought to do this or do that, and was sometimes very explicit about what Pecci should not be doing.

The nuncio paid not too much attention to these messages though he was punctiliously polite in his replies. He knew that above all he wanted to handle one matter—one which would cause no arguments—that of the higher education of Catholics in the country. He encouraged in every way the College of St. Michel in the city, hoping to make it so good that eventually all Catholic education in Belgium could be modeled on it.

In 1834 the Belgian hierarchy had begun the restoration of the University of Louvain which had once had a great reputation. Pecci promised to aid it and when degrees were granted there during his first year in Belgium, he addressed the faculty and students.

"The tradition of the ancient University of Louvain is, I see clearly, still a living one ... I hope you all follow steadfastly the path you have been taught to pursue here," he told the graduates. "It will be for the happiness and honor of Belgium."

Even though the hierarchy was not greatly impressed by
the young envoy, it was clear that King Leopold liked him
very much, seeing in him a scholar, a diplomat, an excellent
priest and a man willing to learn. He liked to propound questions to him and always listened carefully to the answers.
"Monseigneur," the king told Pecci, "you are as clever a
politician as you are an excellent statesman."

Queen Louise also was very fond of him and he found
in her a wonderful understanding of their common Faith.
"Bless my son," she said to him one day, "for I want him to
be a good king some day."

Even in his brief career Archbishop Pecci had become
acquainted with social conditions but hitherto it had been
within the framework of the Holy See. In Belgium he met
with something he had never known before—a new basis of
wealth, one not of birth and inheritance but of commercial
enterprise. All his life had been spent in places where the
concepts of industry were still medieval, just as was the
concept of a ruling class.

In Belgium the new capitalism was already strong. In the
Meuse and Sambre Valleys the products of the mines were
in the hands of a huge industry. Smelting furnaces were being built. The factories were run by steam. Railways helped
spread industry and Belgium was now competing in the
world's markets.

It was clear to the thoughtful young legate that this,
which meant wealth for the country, ought to improve conditions for all its citizens. He was soon to realize that, though
it did improve conditions, the profits came to only a few
while the workers were suffering because they could not
compete with the machine. Handmade products took too
long to make and were too expensive when compared with

the products of the machine. Men and women who worked under the new masters had to accept whatever wages they chose to pay. Even so, many went jobless for machines demanded fewer workers.

The idle were everywhere in Brussels. One third of the people of the city, Pecci was told, were on some form of public relief. At first he had difficulty in understanding this. At Carpineto there were poor people, too, but at least there was work of some kind for all. Here in Brussels it was very different.

At the same time the young legate, having lived all his years in the Papal States and in Rome, was dazzled at coming thus suddenly into the age of machines. Had it not been for the poverty and misery the new life was bringing with it, he would have found it completely enthralling. He had always had a deep interest in science and inventions. Here were things which he, whose study of them had been chiefly in the schoolroom and laboratory, found actually at work in material fact.

In the Papal States there had been no trains. Here were railway lines. He had never even seen a steam train until he came to Brussels. When one day he went with the king and queen to watch them open a new line, he wrote home, "It is part of a miracle—six iron tracks which pass through Belgium in every direction and give the passengers the most comfortable means of travel one can imagine. To come twenty miles in the space of an hour is a miracle. We came from Brussels to Namur in three and a half hours, rushing over a distance of sixty-four miles. Nothing can be more agreeable than to ride in such a fashion at a speed of twenty miles an hour. The most delightful views, villas, villages, castles, pass rapidly on either side like a dream or an optical illusion."

Photography he found equally fascinating. He had always

been interested in the creative sciences and this one held
his close interest. On the occasion of seeing his first pho-
tograph, he wrote a Latin verse about it:

> By pencil of the solar light
> Fair image traced, how deftly thou
> Canst give the transient smile and thought,
> Clear-speaking eye and lovely brow.
>
> Man doth new powers to the sun impart;
> Nature and science here combine,
> Strive here with all but matchless art—
> Apelles' touch must yield to thine.

He was to find Brussels society delightful and he was welcomed in many homes as an honored guest. He was a frequent visitor in the palace for the king invited him on many
occasions. Pecci wrote to Rome that he thought Leopold
was doing his best to take a middle road between the Catholic party and the moderate Liberals and was doing it very
well.

When young Queen Victoria, who was Leopold's niece,
came to Brussels on a state visit, she found the legate from
the Vatican very engaging. The Irish novelist, Charles Lever,
held a salon in the city which drew many into its circle and
Pecci went there occasionally. At the British embassy he met
for the first time the English prelate, Wiseman, a meeting
which was to result in a deep and lasting friendship. Lady
Seymour had a weekly drawing room which Pecci sometimes
attended. It was there that he met the Anglican bishop of
Dublin. The two were mutually attracted and under cover of
the general conversation they talked together all evening,
stopping only to listen to the music which both loved.

Archbishop Pecci had soon discovered that keeping the
peace between the Belgian prelates and himself would be one

of his chief duties. The hierarchy in general was resentful of him and of his friendship with the king, as well as of what they considered his interference with what they considered their prerogatives. Eventually they began to complain to Rome—at one time because the nuncio was inexperienced at dealing with men and affairs, at another because he was not resolute enough in things he could and should handle himself. They felt they were more qualified than he to take care of matters of education. Finally they began suggesting that he might be recalled and someone of the caliber of the former nuncio be appointed. There was a very fine post vacant at Turin.

Of such complaints the nuncio knew nothing, for Cardinal Lambruschini did not tell him. He knew well Pecci's ability and his tact. He knew, too, that it was no simple matter to try to tell bishops how to get along with a ruling group, many of them not Catholics, to say nothing of having to disagree sometimes with the redoubtable cardinal of Malines. Cardinal Lambruschini knew Pecci was no extremist and that he was doubtless handling a difficult situation as well as anyone could.

Archbishop Pecci was of course aware of trouble and occasionally found himself at a loss, as in the case of the Malines cardinal. "He is affable and courteous," Pecci wrote to the secretary of state, "and also tenacious and positive as is the general characteristic of the Flemish." He added that he was carrying out the secretary's injunction to have no friction with the bishops—"and perhaps Rome, too, should not show too much authority too openly."

He knew that this was difficult for himself. He tried hard. Once, caught in a dispute between the University of Louvain and that at Namur, he had refused to say which he thought right, asking to present both claims instead to the Holy See. He was able, however, to carry out one fine thing and with no opposition—the establishment of a college in Rome where Belgian bishops could send their most promising clerics for further study. A vacant monastery had been utilized and in it the Belgian College at Rome opened.

During his years in Belgium the young archbishop learned to practice two qualities—perseverance and patience. They were qualities which were to serve him well in the long years ahead.

By the summer of 1845 complaints against him were becoming stronger. The Austrian ambassador to the Vatican was urging that he be recalled, was in fact demanding it.

A pastoral letter on bad books had just been issued by the hierarchy of Belgium and had greatly provoked the government. "How the government ministers regret the departure of Monsignor Fornari," wrote the ambassador, "who saved situations so often by restraining the higher clergy to a prudent moderation whereas Pecci eclipses himself and seems unwilling to use a moderating influence."

Monsignor Fornari had written from Paris to Pecci urging him to speak out to the bishops, but Pecci, still wary, wrote to Rome that he had given the bishops "my prudent support." At that remark even Lambruschini suggested he follow "not too negative a line of conduct." The nuncio must use his zeal, always regulated by prudence, to uphold the authority of the Holy See "and contain the ardor of these prelates."

Pecci wrote again stating that he had been trying to do just that. He knew by that time that the hierarchy had been annoyed ever since the nunciature had been set up in 1842. Up to that time they had had things all their own way. Nor did it help matters that the cardinal of Malines was very jealous of his own authority and tried to bring forward his higher rank on every possible occasion.

Lambruschini was reluctantly facing the fact that this opposition, which showed no sign of growing less, might become too strong to permit Pecci to carry out his work in Brussels. Yet he was reluctant to have a young prelate on his first diplomatic mission made to look a failure. He knew the insistence against him was coming from those who gave him little chance to do anything constructive.

Then, too, there was in Rome a recently created cardinal, Giacomo Antonelli, who had from the first viewed with alarm this young man whose ideas seemed to him far too liberal for the good of a conservative Church. The hierarchy of Belgium were a little kinder but when they said a good word it was only to damn Pecci with faint praise. He was a good young man but they insisted he knew little of the diplomatic world and when he did take the initiative, it was in the wrong place or at the wrong time. It began to be clear, even to the hesitant Lambruschini, that everything that went wrong would be blamed on the nuncio.

Yet it was difficult to assess exactly what had gone wrong. Pecci had proved a fine administrator in both earlier positions—reforming the customs office, opening saving banks and co-operative granaries, opening evening schools for the sons of workingmen. Several times when there had been meetings of the workers in Brussels, with many Catholics among them, he had gone there to discuss their problems. He had also made friends with many in high places, with the possible exception of most of the hierarchy.

No doubt his reforms were resented by conservatives who saw their own power thus lessened. And it was perhaps true that his limited experience had not been enough to meet the difficulties of the exacting Brussels appointment. Even his French was still imperfect. Then, too, the departure of the previous nuncio had been greatly deplored. It was also true that, given more experience, Pecci would have been better able to handle the difficult hierarchy of Belgium. All these things the secretary of state took into account.

He had also to consider that the post at Belgium was one of great importance to the Vatican. The parliament was divided into Liberal and Catholic party members and the nuncio's chief importance there was that the prime minister of Belgium could count on him to inform his coreligionists regarding tactics these men should espouse. These hints, perhaps, Pecci did not always understand, said his enemies. His friends said it was much more than that. If he did not think the hints should be imparted, he would not do so. In any event, when a coalition of the factions broke down, after it had been carefully prepared, it was Pecci who was blamed.

After long consideration the papal secretary of state came to a decision. By good fortune the bishopric of Perugia was vacant, the bishop having died recently. To Cardinal Lambruschini the opportunity seemed providential, for Perugia had asked if they might have their erstwhile papal governor back as bishop.

Late that year word came from Rome to Archbishop Pecci. He was to be awarded a new position—as the secretary of state made very plain—as a reward for his excellent work in Belgium. He was to receive the see of Perugia which was presently empty. "This appointment," wrote the secretary of state, "shall not in the slightest degree prejudice you in respect to the honors conferred on prelates transferred from a nunciature of the second to one of the first class."

The news of the appointment did not fill Archbishop Pecci with any joy. For one thing this was not a very important see. Perugia was merely a bishopric and he had for several years been an archbishop. His title, he was told, would now be the rather cumbersome one of archbishop-bishop of Perugia. Then, too, he was well aware why he was being taken from Brussels and that it meant the death of his career as a diplo-

mat. The future for which he had prepared for years was
shattered. He knew he was the victim of a manufactured
situation but to many who did not know the story it would
appear that he had been incompetent. This, of course, was
a blow to his pride. Perugia was not the answer for one who
had been hoping for a brilliant career in high places.

He wrote a careful, dignified letter to Rome saying that he
was profoundly moved by this honor of a bishopric but also
was dismayed at receiving it. And, of course, both these
statements were true. It was an honor and he was very
young to have received it. He was hardly thirty-six years old.

King Leopold spoke the feelings of many when he said
that the departure of "so accomplished and skillful a diplomat
grieved him greatly." He spoke, too, of his prudence and his
incorruptibility and decorated him with the Order of Leopold. When the king wrote a letter to the pope about Pecci,
it conveyed more than the words expressed: "I have rarely
met a more sincere devotion, a surer intuition, and more
capable action. I hope when he returns Your Holiness will
ask him for an exact account of his impressions of the affairs
of the Church in Belgium. He judges these things wisely."

Disappointed though he was, the young nuncio played one
diplomatic trick on his enemies in both Belgium and Rome.
He asked to remain in Brussels until spring, chiefly because
his health made a journey in the heart of winter difficult.
There was no doubt some truth in this, but he was also
carrying out a role in which his enemies had said he was
incompetent, that of the astute diplomat. By such a delay
no one could say that he had been summarily dismissed.

Another reason he wished to delay was that a matter had
come up in which the mayor of Louvain, the bishop of that
city and the Jesuits were at odds, and this he was anxious

to see settled since it was a religious and not a political imbroglio.

The Jesuits had a college at Namur. The University of Louvain wanted as many pupils as possible in its college. The cause of religion was not being served well by the arguments which went on between them. The cardinal of Malines had championed the cause of Louvain; it was well known to be the pet project of the Belgian hierarchy. Pecci knew that in the end only Rome could settle the matter entirely and give to each its proper place. It could never find complete settlement in Belgium. At the time neither he nor anyone else knew what would be the end of the controversy. It was settled some years later—and exactly along the lines which the former nuncio had advocated.

In a way this was also to be true regarding his own removal from the nunciature. His disappointment was keen, but later he was to realize what value those years in Belgium had been for him. For one thing, he was young and so had been able to take in many impressions. He had for the first time seen a very different world from the one in which he had grown up. He had been given a fine insight into modern politics, both state and Church, and had learned to defend not only his policies but himself. He had received valuable experience in handling a hierarchy when it had to be done by indirection. And he had been able to view at close hand an example of the new machine age and what it was doing for both the weal and the woe of men—for those of wealth and those of poverty.

When he went to say good-by to the king, the two men exchanged the usual amenities and then the king said to him, "Monseigneur, I'm sorry you were not able to convert me. But even so you are a very winning theologian and I shall ask the pope to give you a cardinal's hat."

"Oh, Your Majesty," said Pecci, "how much more gratifying than receiving the red hat would be the making of an impression on your heart."

"I have no heart," laughed the king.

"Perhaps I should have said—on Your Majesty's mind."

The king grew serious. "On that you have made a very definite impression. I wish you a fine future—and I am sure you will have one."

Since Archbishop Pecci had been told he need not hurry back, he spent, when spring came, some months visiting various cities on his way home, among them Trier where he saw in the ancient cathedral the Holy Coat, supposedly the seamless robe of Christ which Helena had given that city and which was always hidden when danger threatened. He visited Aix-la-Chapelle and the shrine at Fourvière near Lyons.

Queen Louise had given him letters to Louis Philippe of France and his family and he found himself a very welcome guest at the palace. He called on Monsignor Fornari and met with a cordial reception. In Paris he saw to his sorrow how many were being converted to the new creed of socialism which was making such glowing promises to the unemployed and the poor, many of them Catholics. When he reached England he found the same conditions, the same restlessness. Everywhere was increased mechanization. Everywhere were the hungry and homeless, ready to listen to any new doctrine which promised them food and shelter.

The conservatives in France among the clergy evidently had little to offer these people save more faith, more trust in those in power, more resignation to the station in life where

God had placed them. But some who talked with Pecci were uneasy. They saw clearly why the new ideas were finding good ground in which to grow.

"We must defend our convictions of course," one prelate said to him, "but sometimes we must alter our attitudes. These people are after all a part of their country as well as a part of their Faith."

In England Pecci was the guest of the Brazilian ambassador. At the expressed wish of King Leopold he called on "my niece Victoria," and she was very charming to him. He attended a soiree given by Lord Palmerston and saw a great public ceremony in which the queen took part. He attended a court reception. He had a delightful time wandering about London, strolling in the parks. He was very interested in the book and print shops in Pall Mall. He sat in the Distinguished Strangers Gallery in the House of Commons where he heard O'Connell speak. He met and listened to a group of Irish exiles.

Everywhere, even though his visits were made very pleasant, he saw, too, the things that were happening in a changing world. When he reached Rome perhaps his real sadness was not for himself but for what he had witnessed. The machine which had been expected to free the people was only imprisoning them the more in this harsh division of the very rich and the poor. Increased too was his conviction that Catholics must live and grow with the times, that they dared not merely stand aside or find fault. He observed from what he had seen and heard that the Church was, in many high places, not aware of the danger to her own lands or to her own power as a governing state.

He had hoped to tell at least something of all this to the Holy Father but when he reached Rome it was to learn that Gregory had been taken very ill the week before. He was much too sick to receive Pecci and hear from him all the things the latter was so eager to pour out to him, too ill to read the glowing letter from Leopold. He died only a week after Pecci returned home.

To the friends of Archbishop Pecci the death of Pope Gregory was a double loss. They mourned the death of an excellent pontiff. They knew, too, that the pope had planned to create Pecci a cardinal. Now it was feared there might be a long delay about this, especially since they knew that the conservative Cardinal Antonelli would no doubt have a very important place at the papal court. And he was the man who had been very instrumental in the recalling of Pecci from Brussels.

Archbishop Pecci knew the newly elected pope fairly well, having met him in Umbria on several occasions. He was Cardinal Mastai-Ferretti and he took the name of Pius IX.

Chapter Five

SOON after the coronation of Pius IX, Archbishop Pecci, having given a careful account of his mission years to the new pope, left for Umbria. He stopped briefly at Assisi to pray at the tomb of St. Francis. Then he hastened to Perugia for he wanted to reach that city in time to say Mass at the cathedral on the feast of St. Anne, his mother's name day.

He had remained in Rome long enough to witness the first great act of Pius IX—the amnesty that released hundreds of political prisoners from the cells of Roman prisons. The praises to the new and liberal pope were still being voiced everywhere when Pecci left for his episcopal city. He, too, felt in him the glow that was over Rome. This was a pope who wanted to help people, a pope who understood the meaning of justice. Only fifty-four years old, and seeming younger than his years, he was heralded as a progressive and patriotic sovereign, one who would no doubt lead in the movement for the unification of Italy.

Archbishop Pecci returned to Perugia to receive a mighty welcome. Sixty thousand people lined the streets to the cathedral. He rode a white horse. He wore full episcopal regalia. Eight young men held a baldachin over him. Children strewed his way with flowers.

On his first night in his palace the city was illuminated in his honor. Bonfires were lighted and people came, not only from the city but from the villages, to welcome him back. It was more than evident that they remembered him with deep affection and that the welcome was genuine. To him the spontaneous outburst of affection was heart-warming.

The problems which faced him in Perugia were those of any diocese in Italy at the time. No doubt chief among them was that of education, both lay and clerical, and for both boys and girls. Another was the presence in Perugia, as well as in other cities, of the forces of socialism and the Enlightenment that were working to win over the people. Perugia was no longer a harmonious, one-minded, one-hearted community.

There was one weapon which could be used against them —education—as much and as good as it was possible to provide. The archbishop chose to give much time and effort to creating schools, to raising the standards in the seminaries, to sending out pastoral letters which people could understand.

What he especially needed was a clergy alive to the dangers inherent in the well-disciplined secular forces; priests who would take up the cause of the people and win them back to the Faith and hold them in it, who would make people know that the Church was with them and not against their freedom and their interests.

The diocesan seminary was close to his palace. Founded in 1571 and never enlarged, it was far too small. His first plan had been to rebuild or at least to add a wing. But, since money was a thing to be carefully considered, he decided to house the overflow in a wing of his palace. Of course, even altering meant considerable financing and during the next years he used much of his own income for this work. He recognized how antiquated was the system of studies and so he greatly increased the curriculum. He created new departments and invited distinguished scholars to head them.

Along with this work of education he continued to concern himself with lesser matters. Of his students and his professors he demanded strict discipline. For months the story was told of the day Don Brunelli was late for his class, due to a mix-up in appointments. When he came into the room, he found His Excellency calmly explaining a passage from the Oration for Milo. When Don Brunelli sat down among his students the substitute teacher rose to give up his place but the professor asked him to continue to the end of the hour. The archbishop smilingly shook his head and withdrew.

"Perhaps the warm smile he gave me was a tacit but amiable reproval," Don Brunelli would say when he told the story on himself. "If so it was a very pleasant kind of reproof."

The archbishop of Perugia lived a very simple life. He worked hard and studied continually. He read voraciously and his study looked like a library reading room with books, magazines and papers strewn everywhere. His desk was always littered and no one was allowed to touch it. His secretary groaned when one day the bed was covered, too.

Over the years Pecci had made many friends in various cities. When any of these men passed through Perugia or came close to it, they were accustomed to stop off to visit him, but always quietly, some of them almost secretly. There was no fanfare or public entertaining during these visits—"so Antonelli won't get jealous," whispered the gossips. For Cardinal Antonelli was now secretary of state, with a power even greater than had been his under Gregory.

Cardinal Antonelli obviously did not expect any trouble with Pecci now: he was safely placed in a bishopric. But it was good for the archbishop to have these friendly contacts which gave him a knowledge of what was going on in many places, both governmental and papal.

As in his other missions, he carried out here his special devotions—to the Sacred Heart, to Our Lady, to St. Joseph. He rose at daybreak and set to work after an early Mass which was followed by a cup of coffee and a roll. He ate only one real meal a day—soup, meat, salad and cheese with fruit. "The enemy of delicacies," said one of his friends.

His avocation, and a beloved one, was the study of Dante. To this much of his leisure was devoted. Thomas Aquinas, too, he read more and more as time went on. He knew him well from his long years at school with the Jesuits. St. Ignatius enjoined his sons to make Thomistic philosophy the basis of their studies in philosophy and theology. But Pecci's reading was more an application of the great scholar's ideas to the present times. The more he read the Angelic Doctor, the more he grew eager to bring him from the dimness of old libraries into the light of every day where, he felt, his great theories would be of use to a world growing more and more troubled and puzzled, more and more involved in ever greater material inventions and improvements and at the same time faced by a more and more impoverished working class.

Aquinas he studied, but Dante he loved. He could recite whole cantos of his poetry by heart. In later years, when he was a very old man, friends would sometimes quote a line, hoping for once to trip him by reciting one he did not remember. He always picked it up and went on to finish the canto.

One of the first things he learned to his horror when he came back to Perugia was that the seminarians were not allowed to read Dante. He immediately took away the penalties from those who had been caught reading him secretly and hiding the books under their mattresses. Sometimes he read the great poet with them and explained those passages not clear to them.

He encouraged the young men in their study of literary and scientific subjects. He was very proud of those who could write good verse in Latin and went over it with them for better choice of words and for scansion. He restored the teaching of philosophy, and always along the lines of St. Thomas. For help in this he often consulted his learned Jesuit brother, now teaching in Rome.

Later he founded at Perugia the Academy of St. Thomas for the younger clergy. There they could earn additional degrees. He explained clearly his purpose—to demonstrate that all discoveries and investigations of modern science could and should be examined in the light of the sound Christian philosophy of St. Thomas.

He reorganized the University of Perugia and the Collegio della Sapienza. He raised the standard of the seminary until it was considered one of the best in Italy. He was himself one of the examiners at the seminary examinations. It was his delight that during the vacations his palace became a gathering place for students of the Belgian college in Rome, for many had known him in Brussels and stopped to see him on their way home.

The archbishop did not confine his educational works only to higher education. Over the years he set up a free school for little girls and an academy for older girls and invited as teachers the Religious of the Sacred Heart. He built a large school for them, aware that girls as well as boys needed a competent education. He set up what he named the Gardens of St. Philip Neri where on Sundays children could come to receive religious instruction and also to play games.

He opened a House of Providence and placed it under the direction of the Belgian Sisters of Providence. He opened a home for poor women who suffered from chronic diseases and also a foundling home which he placed under the Franciscan Sisters. He built an orphanage for boys and one for girls and saw to it that both had competent teachers.

He also opened night schools for young workers where, under the care of the Oratorian Fathers, men and boys could come after work. He set up the Society of St. Joachim for priests who were old and poverty stricken.

These were all matters for his flock, but sometimes he made political moves, too. In 1849, when the Garibaldians were raising havoc in Perugia and the Austrians were ready to stop them by entering the city Pecci knew that such a move could easily stir the Perugians to revolt. He went himself to the Austrian camp and succeeded in dissuading them from an attack.

The news which came to Perugia during the first year of Pecci's return was good news. Evidently the new pope was taking things into his own hands. There had been, years before his election, a long and unreasonable delay in giving him the red hat, due, people said, to his liberal tendencies. Therefore, the fact that he, and not a known conservative, had been elected, was received with great interest and in some places with joy. He was acknowledged to be a man of charity, of good heart and also one with a fine wit. People knew that he thought the Papal States were in need of some reform and that he planned to do this in his own way, for he had been greatly annoyed at having France and Austria give continual advice to the papal authorities on how to change things.

Pius IX had been in office less than a year when he relaxed censorship laws, replaced the municipal army with a civil guard and set up a municipal militia for Rome. He planned a cabinet of heads of departments and announced that the

secretary of state, who was to lead it, was the only one who
needed to be a cleric. In fact, in the beginning there were
four laymen on the council. To govern Rome itself he planned
an elected body, representative of varying political opinions.

These were moderate reforms and in keeping with the
times. But before long it was clear that he would not be able
to carry out his program. It had grown too late for papal
reforms. Pius' hopes were shattered by the radical element
which was beginning to dominate Rome and other parts of
the world. The last thing in the world that the Risorgimento
or, indeed, any of the revolutionaries, wanted, was a reform
pope.

The country was aflame with revolutionary and with national fervor. The tenets of the Enlightenment, espoused by
many, were a denial of ancient convictions. During the Ren-
aissance and the Reformation the great majority had belief
in the supernatural, but now reason was to be enthroned
and reason worshipped. Religions would have to go as, said
Schopenhauer, "a nurse leaves the child which has outgrown
her fostering care." Some Catholics, too, were seduced by this
joy of forming one's own opinions on everything, including
one's faith. Some of them were to leave their Church. Others
were merely strengthened in their faith.

It was not his fault that Pius failed. The year 1848, one
of revolution, with radical after radical rising to foment new
ones, put an end to the moral reforms he had hoped to establish. Garibaldi had at first been sympathetic to his plan
of government but the revolutionary party was not. When
Pius' minister of state, Count Rossi, was killed by revolution-
ists, the horrified pope withdrew his plans entirely. He did
not want to win success through bloodshed.

In that same year he was forced to flee Rome in disguise
and take refuge at Gaeta, in the kingdom of Naples, where
he remained for two years. When he was able to return, it

was by grace of the French forces of Napoleon III. He came home to find that a temporary revolt had declared an end of papal power. The revolt was overcome only with the help of a French armed force.

The Pius who came back to Rome was very different from the one who had fled two years before. When elected, he was well aware of the spirit of the times and had been to some extent sympathetic. He realized he was living in an era of discoveries in the material world, a time productive of inquiry which would foster doubt unless it was controlled. He had been a true liberal who had fought the false liberalism of socialism.

Now he was greatly changed. In addition he had as his secretary of state Cardinal Antonelli who, even the kindest critic would agree, was a man of medieval views and an ultraconservative. He was also a career man. He had never been ordained a priest but was really a civil administrator and he was to be the last of the career secretaries. Then, too, his private life was not of the highest moral tone, something which was proved when he died. He had made a large fortune, and it was willed to his natural children.

Pius no longer had any thought of planning reforms for the Papal States. It was of course too late now even to discuss this for many Italians were filled with one idea—the unification of Italy—and for this he was not needed. Two things were clear, however—Pius would refuse to part with even the smallest portion of the papal properties. On the other hand, if papal ideas stood in the way of uniting the country, the advocates of unification would certainly push them aside.

To a certain, even to a considerable, degree, the archbishop of Perugia was in full agreement with the pope and his close associates in Rome. His pastoral letters to his own people reflected that. He was with the more liberal group

at the papal court, however, in realizing that changing times
demanded changing viewpoints.

On December 17, 1853, at a consistory, Archbishop Pecci
was created cardinal. All the diplomatic corps and the Italian
nobility were present, as well as a deputation from Perugia.
They thanked the pope for the honor to their city, and took
the new cardinal home proudly.

Even now, when, after long delay, the cardinal's hat was
given him, he was not invited to remain in Rome. Cardinal
Antonelli, who knew the reforming ideas of Pecci, should
also have known—and perhaps he did—that Pecci did not
think all progress was necessarily good or even necessary.
In fact, at an episcopal synod Pecci had suggested the Holy
See put forth a condemnation of the "errors of the age." On
the other hand, he would never have agreed that all progress
was error, and perhaps that was his crime in Antonelli's eyes.
At any rate, there was little doubt that Antonelli, perhaps
because he knew a reformer was incurable, was the prime
factor in keeping Pecci at a distance. So the newly named
cardinal could only look on from afar while his beloved country split into groups of nationalistic patriots, engaging in
revolutionary activity and holding to a constantly narrowing
viewpoint as to what belonged to the papacy and what belonged to the country.

When Cardinal Pecci returned to his palace the city gave
him a fine welcome. Many came in person to honor the man
who for the past years had worked so hard for them. Bands
heralded his procession to the cathedral as he passed through
the ancient gates of the city and rode through decorated
streets to the cathedral square hung with tapestries.

He pontificated and then preached, and though some of
his sermon was of the future, part of it was of the immediate

past and of the present, of the earthquake which had the week before his return wrought great damage to the city and had created a near famine.

Fortunately he had, some years before, created grain stores to be held for just such an emergency as this. Because these had been so recently set up there was not yet a sufficient surplus to provide for all the needy, and so he opened in the episcopal palace a free kitchen for the poor. There some received raw supplies to take home. Others were given bread and hot soup.

"My mother used to do this," he said one day, looking over the ample supplies, some the gifts of people in the city, some his own. "She would be happy if she could see it."

One day someone in the crowd asked, "Do his clergy in that big palace ever keep anything to eat for themselves?"

By 1860 Cavour, then premier of Sardinia, and the moving force in suggesting the first king for a united Italy, agreed to cede Nice to France. In return he was promised a free hand in Italy, with the exception of Rome itself. A new papal army was hastily formed but the united forces of Sardinia's king with the help of Garibaldi and his men found it no difficult matter to defeat them. The Papal States, many of them the gift to the papacy of Pepin the Short in the eighth century, were gone. The Patrimony of Peter—Rome itself and its immediate environs—was now all that remained to the pope and even that he owed in great measure to the help of the army of Napoleon III. Pius was left to carry on his rule in the one place left him. No liberalism remained in him now. Even a tinge of it seemed dangerous.

During this difficult time there were within the Church liberal-minded men speaking out. In France Bishop Dupanloup and Montalembert were expounding the theory of a free church in a free state. In Germany Dr. Döllinger was demanding the right of a scholar to make independent research, to listen to the viewpoints of the opposition.

Pius had not spoken on such matters for some time. When he did so it was in no uncertain terms. He wrote an encyclical in which he denounced his opponents and said they were trying to "eliminate every idea of faith and truth." Annexed to the paper was a syllabus which listed "the eighty principal errors of our time." Many of them were not new and had been condemned by other popes at various times. About these there was no real dispute. It was only that now they were listed in a group and in one place. The really important "error" was the last named—that a Roman pontiff should ever be expected to reconcile himself to or agree to reconcile himself with liberalism, modern progress and modern civilization.

Many who read this were aghast. For here, and at a most critical time, came a blow to Catholic liberalism which boded ill for the immediate future and perhaps even for the more distant future of the Church.

Cardinal Pecci, when asked his opinion, said he thought the syllabus was not directed against science but rather against atheism, that a careful reading would show it was against present evils, and nothing more. He said no more about it but he did not by any means remain silent regarding the events of 1860. In February he sent out a pastoral letter on the subject of the temporal dominion of the pope, in which he tried to clarify matters for his own people.

He spoke of past history and of present-day difficulties, of the divine principles of holiness and truth which could not be subject to any earthly power. "The Church is the kingdom of Christ. Can the head of this kingdom become the subject of a mere earthly potentate? Civil power is charged

with peace and security and order; the Church has for its
function to direct humanity towards its supernatural destiny
. . . One cannot make the Roman Pontiff the subject of any
earthly power."

It was a powerful piece of writing. It ended, "There is no
middle course. Either we have to stand faithful to Christ, to
His Church, to that Church's visible head and against the
enemies of our religion—or take part with them against God
and His Church. It is no longer a matter of policy. It is a
matter of conscience. We cannot continue to hesitate between God and Belial."

With other papal principalities Perugia had fallen to the
United Kingdom of Italy in 1860, when 15,000 Piedmontese
troops took the city. Perugia and all Umbria were annexed
to Piedmont.

This betokened a great change for the church in Perugia.
Cardinal Pecci must in future do much of his dealing with
men who had only contempt for the Church and who wanted
her to have nothing to do or say about the education of her
children. It also meant that the teaching sisters and brothers
were driven away and Pecci had to find replacements. As
partial aid he organized the Union of Preachers of the Word
of God, priests who went everywhere in the diocese where
they were called and gave religious teaching to the children
and preached to the grown people.

A newly appointed commissioner had replaced the former
papal delegate. He proceeded to close monasteries, to sanc-
tion civil marriages, to open lay schools. When the city was
occupied by Italian troops, the cardinal was told he must
give lodging in his palace to General Carini. He agreed and
gave his own rooms to the general. The latter, coming to

thank him, found him in a small room and realized the cardinal had given up his own apartment. He refused it and went to a hotel.

This led to their becoming friends. One day the general asked him to visit a young garrison captain who was dying and had asked for a priest. The young man smiled when he saw the black-clad form coming to his bed. Pecci stayed with him a long time, talking softly and keeping the dying boy's hand in his own. He did not leave him until death came.

There was little Pecci could do now save work for his own diocese and among his clergy, and see that the teaching of the seminarians went on as well as possible. The Piedmontese had taken the seminary for their own use but the cardinal said his staff needed only a few rooms. He opened the seminary in his palace and there they all lived.

He did not complain about the many things with which he could not agree and which he saw going on; it would have done no good. For the time being it was best for all concerned to carry out their religious duties and remain silent on many matters, but not on all. Some things he could not ignore. During the next few years he wrote eighteen protests against the actions of the conquerors and spoke very plainly. Only once did he get into trouble with the new authorities. In 1862 he told his people not to support the "patriot priests" several of whom he had penalized for yielding unduly in their religious principles. One took his case to court and the cardinal was arrested. It was a very brief arrest and he was acquitted. To have a cardinal in jail was not anything even the zealous authorities wanted.

On this matter of the so-called patriot priests, as the government press and the admiring rulers called them, he complained to the Royal Commissary, expressing his "formal reprobation and profound pain." It brought about no change, and with a heavy heart he wrote again, when all monastic orders were dispersed and their property seized, "A law which aims at social justice itself, besides wounding religion. I condemn by my pastoral liberty this decree and in all its parts."

On this matter he appealed to the king, but with no results. He sent him at various times nine such protests, all expressed in courteous terms, but he was never given the return courtesy of an answer. He could not give aid to the impoverished monks and religious from his own scanty funds. Most of his resources had been seized by the new masters of Italy, but he managed to spend less himself in order to give the dispossessed a little help.

When the girls' school at Perugia which he had founded was taken by the government, Cardinal Pecci, in a letter both sad and indignant, wrote to the king once more. Only three years before he had managed to build it, he wrote, and now the little girls whom it sheltered had been thrown out. Also sad, and also brought to the king's attention, was the expulsion of the monks of Camaldoli, whom an ancestor of the king, as Pecci pointed out, had given a place for their monastery in 1700: "They are now made the object of ignoble calumny and, with only eight days notice, driven from the sanctuary they had themselves built—men separated from the worldly pursuits by prayer and silence, men whom the world never saw coming from their high mountain save when brotherly charity compelled them and whose convent was the refuge of the pilgrim, the sick, the poor—these are held up as imperiling the interests of the nation."

Instead of growing less, the depredations grew worse until not only the congregations of men but also those of women were despoiled of their lands and belongings. This meant that many of them, who had always been able to take care of their communities without help, were now thrown on the charity of their neighbors.

One of the worst tragedies was one which Cardinal Pecci worked hard to avert. It was that of Don Santi, parish priest of San Donato, whom he knew to be a kindly and gentle man and whom the new regime accused of shooting an Italian officer by firing a gun at him through a window of the rectory.

Dressed as a simple priest, the cardinal went from one authority to another, trying to save Don Santi's life. He gave strong proofs of his innocence but they were ignored. The court simply said that sentence had been passed and the priest must be executed. He was, despite the insistence that he was not the murderer. Months later it was learned that he really had been innocent. The killer, on his death bed, confessed the crime.

Even though it brought no results, Pecci continued his complaints, to local authorities on matters in Perugia, and directly to the king on such matters as the new decree on marriage (making it civil only), on the expulsion of orders, the gradual occupation of everything in the Papal States. In 1864 he sent a spirited objection to King Victor Emmanuel regarding the wholesale drafting of priests and seminarians into the army: "In the grief of our souls we cannot believe that such liberty should be taken in such a matter. Put a stop, Sire, to these laws which succeed one the other, and all in injury to the Church—and an injury which will eventually rebound to the state too."

Sometimes the only thing he could do about some of these unjust laws was give in to some degree. That was what he did when it was learned that, by paying a heavy tax, young men could be released from military service. The cardinal formed a committee which contributed funds for this purpose and some seminarians were thus spared to remain at their studies. As for the old and superannuated priests, his Society of St. Joachim took care of them.

In 1864 during Lent he addressed a pastoral to his people—"people like you who have the fortune to be born Catholics. Listen now while the free and loving voice of your pastor warns you of this one thing especially: learn to distinguish between good education and that which calls itself good but is far from being so." And he spoke with special sadness of the children, of the secular education which was now all that many of them received—"and innocence thus receives wounds which time can never cure."

He knew that the words in his letters to the king would have no effect even though he was addressing a professedly Catholic monarch. In March of 1863 a royal edict had been published by Victor Emmanuel in which he spoke of the Holy See as "a foreign power" and announced that by royal decree all clerical appointments were void unless first submitted to the king's authorities and confirmed by them.

Even though Pecci knew the gesture was futile, he sent a protest: "Such an edict opens the door to party intrigue, to the favoring of disobedient and worldly minded priests, to the giving of subsidies to the few suspended priests while the law-abiding are left penniless."

Every bishop in Umbria signed it.

Chapter Six

P IUS IX was exhibiting more and more clearly his own intention and that of the conservatives about him, as well as of a part of the Church outside Italy. His intent was so to centralize the authority of the Church that in future she would never again be in danger of an attempted control by a secular state—and that of course meant Italy.

He knew exactly how he meant to do it. It was an idea promulgated before but always minimized by the more liberal element, as they did now when word of his intention came to their ears. His plan was to define a dogma, one long accepted but never actually defined, that of the infallibility of the pope when he spoke on faith or morals. It was made clear that such a formal definition was to be confined to times when the pontiff made ex-cathedra pronouncements, and that these were infallible because they took their authority from God and not with the consent of the Church.

The matter was discussed for some years. As early as 1862 Pius had announced his intention of calling a council. By 1868 this intention had become a certainty. One thing was very clear. Though other matters would be discussed, the chief reason for holding the council was to discuss and to define a dogma of infallibility. It was also obvious that this would be no simple matter. Opposition was being voiced both by heads of governments and by individual Catholics, as well as by interested Protestants.

Gladstone said that seemingly Rome was polishing up tools people thought had been put aside. Catholics in England, men like Lord Acton and Dr. Newman, called the bill untimely, for they felt it was being introduced at a very impolitic hour. The American hierarchy, with very few exceptions, were also against promulgating it at that special time. It was unfortunate, too, that Pius only two years before had proscribed American Protestant worship on strictly Roman soil. The result was that President Johnson had replied by ordering the American diplomatic mission to the Holy See closed. There had been a legate there since 1848, when President Polk, in a message to Congress, had asked for the expenses of opening diplomatic relations with the Holy See and the Papal States. It had been approved by both houses, with the understanding that this appointment was with the pope as a temporal ruler only. Pius' prestige had been high in the United States and he seemed definitely one who would take a lead in promoting political reforms in Italy.

During the Civil War the Confederacy had sent a delegation to try to bring papal sympathy to their cause, but the minister plenipotentiary, Rufus King, representing the Union, was able to counter that. However, by that time the Papal States were no longer an important temporal power and since the mission to Rome had been set up by the United States purely for reasons of state, when Rufus King was recalled in 1868 no one was sent to replace him.

In Italy, at Naples, a Freethinkers group was greatly annoyed that the Catholic Church should hold a council at all—"in this age of enlightenment and progress." But theirs was a world where science was the basis of all knowledge

and to them dogma based on revelation was nothing but an
outworn superstition of the past.

In Switzerland protest meetings were held. From France
came clerical protests, expressing the fear that this would
raise high barriers between the faithful. And English Anglicans said Rome did not seem to realize how badly this would
affect a world where the light of faith was already low.

In Germany Dr. Döllinger had been trying to delay the
opening of the council through Bavarian ecclesiastics who
objected to having the dogma promulgated at that time.
Prince Hohenlohe, whose brother was a cardinal, also objected. The prince was appointed to the Holy See but when
he arrived Pius refused to see him at all. However, a much
more important objection came from Bishop von Ketteler of
Mainz who came to ask the pope to delay the matter of the
dogma. "Save the Church of God," he begged. In fact, only
the Spanish and South American hierarchies spoke in complete favor of the measure.

In general, the objections all stemmed not from the dogma
itself, long accepted by Catholics, but the ratifying of it at
that difficult time.

The council—the first held since that of Trent in the sixteenth century—opened December 8, 1869. From all parts
of the world came cardinals, patriarchs, bishops, abbots. The
oldest was eighty-five years old. The youngest was thirty-
five—Bishop Gibbons from the United States. Among them
was Cardinal Pecci who had left Perugia to take his place
at the council just after he had sent out his letter to the
civil authorities regarding the matter of drafting clerical
students for military service, a law which, he wrote, was
"a pitiless ax laid at the roots of the Church's nursery."

On the appointed day of opening the Fathers of the Council entered St. Peter's in a long procession, last of all the pope, high on his sedia. The bearers stopped before the altar of the Tomb of Peter and the pope stepped down and stood for a moment in silent prayer. Then his clear voice began to chant the Veni Creator Spiritus and all joined in.

When this was ended, they all moved to the right transept and took their places, the pope on a throne facing them. The only members of the laity present were the representatives of the temporal rulers who thus made use of their ancient privilege of being present at church councils.

There were lesser matters to be discussed and these were settled with little delay. It was very evident that all were waiting for the one great matter to be presented and discussed. It was to be no swiftly settled thing. The discussions went on for a long time, for there was considerable opposition from France, Germany and the United States. Not until the following July was it actually put to a vote and the first vote showed 451 in favor and 88 opposed, while 62 wanted it made less definite.

The last of the many votes came on a day in July, one of oppressive heat. As the voting began a thunderstorm burst over Rome. Lightning flashed at the windows. Thunder rolled and all but drowned the voices as the prelates registered their *placet* or *non placet* through the peals.

When the voting was finished the storm was still raging and the basilica was very dark. By the light of a candle held close to the paper he had in his hand, the pope read: "And having been approved by this sacred council, we confirm and define. . . ."

Even during the Te Deum and the benediction which followed, the storm continued. Coming from the building, a *London Times* reporter was heard to say to the man beside him, "It made me feel that the God of the Old Testament was there."

The final vote had been all but unanimous, but there were fewer votes than there had been, for some members had gone home. The vote of 533 to 2 (one of the dissenting votes from the United States, the other from Italy) was a triumph of sorts for Pius IX. He was well aware that some governments had opposed it, no doubt because it would lessen their interference with what papal rights were left the pope. In France, for instance, it would weaken and perhaps destroy the power of Gallicanism, the long standing theory that a French monarch had special rights in the Church.

Despite all the difficulties it might cause in the future, it had one very valuable result. The final accord, the all but universal agreement after months of argument, would have its effect on the outside world. It showed that there was a deep and basic unity in the governance of the Church.

There were some sad results. Men left the Church in consequence, among them Père Hyacinthe, the very popular Notre Dame preacher, who founded what he called the "Gallican Church," and Dr. Döllinger in Germany, who formed the Old Catholic Church and took with him many of his powerful friends. And there were others in other lands.

There were national results, too. Austria annulled its concord with the Vatican which had lasted fifteen years. In France the monarchist element, predominant among the hierarchy, loudly protested its adherence to the papacy. In Germany some felt it was one cause of the Kulturkampf which broke out soon afterward, though many felt the council was only very indirectly to blame for the later hardships suffered by Catholics in that country.

The really surprising fact which emerged was how few actually did leave the Church. Some who had spoken their opinions loudly agreed with the dogma, once it had been passed, even those who, actuated by liberal leanings, had also been actuated by a fear that the Church would do herself more harm than good by voting on it at that disturbed time.

Pius IX did not have much time or chance to enjoy his victory, for new events soon spoiled it for him. France, whose soldiers had kept secure his holdings in and about Rome during the past years, now had to recall them. There was a war on with Prussia and France would need all her armies for that conflict.

As a consequence, in September of 1870 Italian troops took over the city of Rome. The Italian government said this was done to "maintain order" although the fact was that the pope had enough troops to meet any inner trouble. On September 19 he stood at the very top of the Scala Santa—which he had climbed on his knees—and addressed his troops in the piazza of the Lateran. Then he went back to the Vatican and remained there. That night the bombardment began, but it did not last long for the pope had given orders to make only a token resistance, enough to show that he was yielding to force and unwillingly. Next day the papal Zouaves were disbanded. Early the next year the government of the Kingdom of Italy was moved from Florence to Rome, the new capital of Italy.

It had all been done, so to speak, legally. An election had been held in the city and it had been overwhelmingly voted that Rome be incorporated into the new kingdom. The king had written the pope asking him to forego all claim to the Papal States—and this time it meant Rome itself—and Pius had refused. The fighting ended when a white flag was hoisted on the dome of St. Peter's as a token of surrender.

Indemnity for the pope had also been carefully worked out, a settlement for the heavy losses in buildings as well as in power. It was a sorry settlement about which the pope had not even been asked an opinion. He was to be paid the sum of three million lire annually for the possessions now taken from the Church. He was to keep the Vatican palace and a small area surrounding it, as well as St. Peter's. The rest of Rome—lands and palaces and buildings—was to belong henceforth to the state. It was a final and complete separation of Church and state. It was the beginning of the end of the papacy as a political power. But even then there were people who were insisting that loss of the Papal States and the Roman Palace, even of the Quirinal, did not mean that the spiritual power of the papacy had ended because the material power was gone.

Pius, in a gesture of defiance, refused the lire which had been offered and also refused to give up his claim to the Papal States. He withdrew to the Vatican, announcing that he would not leave it until this evil deed was undone.

Cardinal Pecci had taken no active part in the public debates. Rather he had been, as Gibbons said later of Cardinal McCloskey, "a silent Solon." But he had been a striking figure there and his affable ways, his ability as a conversationalist, had made him stand out. Though he offered no arguments, his learning and his administrative experience were felt. Years later, Cardinal Gibbons said he thought it excellent that Pecci had not been much involved, for when, a few years later, he took the highest office of all, it was in peace and concord with all shades of theological opinion.

Back again in Perugia after the council was over, he continued his life as usual. If he was weary of the interminable years he spent in this one place, he concealed it, even though there were times when he knew a deep frustration. He had of course known from the beginning why he had been sent to Perugia—the ultraconservatives at Rome wanted to prove he had failed in the Belgian mission and so was of no value for diplomatic office. He knew why he was kept from Rome—

certain cardinals wanted no chance of his influencing the pope who, it was known, held a warm affection for Pecci.

He knew, too, that to be a bishop and an archbishop and a cardinal were high honors even though he knew that those same men in Rome considered these honors bestowed not for good work but in spite of his work. Ever since the ambitious young prelate had gone to Perugia he had known it meant the end of a promising career, ended almost before it began. And he knew that it was one powerful man at the Vatican who kept him where he was.

Through the years he had sent letters to the pope regarding matters in which he expressed an opinion. Once, for example, he wrote on how to bring about a greater unity among the bishops—there was no reply. Perhaps the pope had never seen it. In 1850 he had written Pius suggesting the Church get the co-operation of intelligent and trustworthy laymen to help him. There was no reply.

His friends from Rome who came to visit him on their way to other assignments told him plainly that it was unlikely that anything he sent the Holy Father would be brought to his attention. Cardinal Antonelli had been heard to say— and more frequently of late—that Pecci was still trying to interfere with matters that were none of his business but which were solely the concern of the secretary of state.

In 1857 Pius had made a visitation of provinces of the Papal States. Archbishop Pecci had written him various pieces of information about Perugia so that he would better know the conditions there before he arrived. The answer to his letter came from Cardinal Antonelli and it told him very plainly that he was not to take on himself any initiative of this sort, even if it was only indirectly political.

Years later, when both Pius and Antonelli were dead and Leo was the reigning pope, a man who was planning, and with the pope's permission, to write a life of him, referred

to those unanswered letters. "I got no reply because Antonelli did not wish it," said Leo. "But let us not talk about
it for it distresses me too much. Had it not been for him I
think the pope would not today find himself in such a difficult position at times."

In Rome many had watched this once politically eager man
who had been relegated to the background by some of his
peers. During later years his opinions had been read and
listened to and respected by many. It was known that the
Italian government, though completely anticlerical, respected
him and was interested in his pastoral letters and also in the
excellent results in his diocese. He had over the years built
thirty-six churches and had restored many others. He had
worked hard to raise the intellectual as well as the spiritual
tone of his seminarians.

Some of his pastorals had been given very special attention, such as the one on the claims of the papacy to temporal
sovereignty. His feeling was that it was based on a "hierarchy of ends" and on the organization of the world as established by God. Without such temporal rights the pope
would be a subject of whatever power at any time was the
ruling one, kindly or inimical. "He who must look after the
highest end, the spiritual, cannot in reason be the subordinate of those who are working for material ends," he wrote.

Though he to some degree agreed with Dupanloup's views
on social reform regarding Church and state in Italy, yet
in 1870 he stood firmly against the loss of the papal empire
and the confiscation of the property of religious orders as
well.

Once, when the then premier Rattazzi was passing through
Perugia, he came with his wife to call on the cardinal. Signora Rattazzi wrote home that she had greatly liked the

prelate: "The chief impression he makes is one of asceticism but that is offset and softened by the affection with which he unbends to children. He is no ordinary person," she wrote.

Cardinal Pecci's silver anniversary as a prelate occurred in 1871. He felt that the situation in the Church was too sad to celebrate such an occasion, but the people insisted. A procession took place in his honor, a long stream of people marching around old San Lorenzo Cathedral, carrying banners and singing.

The Piedmontese who now ruled the city did not interfere with the procession to the cathedral which was, said the older among the observers, the longest ever seen in the city. The most important thing about the celebration of his day was, the cardinal thought, the fact that all day the Blessed Sacrament was exposed in the cathedral and priests and people came in crowds to visit and to pray.

In 1874 the pope suggested appointing Pecci to a position in Rome but Antonelli was alert and Pecci remained in Perugia. In the next year, however, the pope suggested to him that he give up his see and accept one at Frascati. Then he would be closer to him as well as to Rome. The cardinal was well aware that there were many implications in this offer. The pope had given him a free hand about accepting; it was not a command. In the end Pecci decided to remain at Perugia, to the joy of his people.

Four years later the pope appointed him protector of the Third Order of St. Francis and in November he took possession of this charge in a ceremony at Assisi. He spoke to the assembled thousands in a voice full of emotion. "From childhood I have been devoted to this great saint," he said, and hoped the tertiaries would through him "become instruments in re-establishing on earth the quiet we have lost and the peace we long for so eagerly and which he knew so well."

He still found time in his busy life for Dante and also for an occasional verse of his own. These were not so much classical themes now as personal, as this short poem at the death of Don Pietro Penna, a holy old man and much loved, shows:

> All this life's lovely way
> No whiter soul, more true, more kind
> In all the country one could find;
> In happy days or harsh always he was
> The pastor kind, the joy of his flock.

And of another unselfish priest:

> Always he heard the cries of need of his own fold;
> And though he was so poor, he gave them gold.

There were others not so kind, one of them dedicated to a certain "Gallus, a gentleman of Perugia," evidently a rather dissolute type whom Pecci was trying to recall to a good life by showing him his past—and his future. It began,

> A boy with downy cheeks in whom burned fires lit by Chloe;
> A man—and to fan the fire Bice and Corinna now conspire;
> A graybeard, ready still to caress Nigella's neck.

"Is there no end to this?" the poem inquired, and implied there was and that the end would not be a happy one unless a change came.

Early in 1877 Pius IX was taken very ill. Aware that he might die, he came to an unusual decision. Because the Holy See was now involved in so many difficulties and because this next election would be the first held after the loss of papal properties, he planned to allow the cardinals to discuss his possible successor.

Now for the first time it was learned how many had known and appreciated Pecci over the years, for his name was suggested by several cardinals before that of anyone else. Cardinal Manning was one who spoke up strongly for him. Antonelli, of course, brushed aside the very mention of his name and Cardinal Randi said he would give his vote only to a nobleman like Chigi or a saint like Martinelli.

It was apparent that the College of Cardinals was equally divided on the matter of what kind of pope the times demanded. Some thought it should be, at so critical a time in the fortunes of the Church, one who would introduce no new ideas; what was needed was a man who prayed a great deal and who could be counted on to do very little else. Leave things as they are and put the Church in the hands of Providence, they said.

But others—called by some at the papal court the "anti-Antonellis"—laughed this idea to scorn. The need of the day was to get into situations, not merely to stay out of them. The deepest need was to see that the social order so evidently establishing itself would have a Christian imprint, one which the Church alone could give.

The pope listened to their opinions but offered few of his own. Pius IX gave very few opinions now on any subject. He met the world chiefly through prelates and the occasional audiences to pilgrims, for he was too ill to see large audiences. He spent much of his time in his Bath chair. The mind within the tired body remained very active, however, and so did his feelings regarding the state of the world. "I am tired of the many injustices," he said, "and I shall not lay down my arms."

There was little doubt that even he now realized that the

Church must meet some changes actively and not merely oppose them. When he was asked if he had any advice to leave for the next pope, he shook his head. "No. Everything I know and knew has changed," he said, "and I am too old now to change my own orientation."

His was to be the longest reign of any pope and the last years were embittered and sad. He watched the world living what to him was an always more wildly wrong life and one ever more lawless. He saw the Kulturkampf, which involved chiefly the matter of Catholic education, overwhelm the Church in Germany and he knew that Bismarck said it was the pope's insistence on his dogma that had fired it.

The pope, never at a loss for return remarks, had said that the Church in Germany was suffering again as she had ages ago. He called Bismarck a second Nero and a modern Attila. He issued an encyclical condemning the war in Germany against the Church, but few in power in the various governments of Europe were listening now to the angry frustrated man at the Vatican, the prisoner, said someone, "only of his own obstinacy." It was an unfair remark for later and more liberal popes were to remain prisoners, too, and he had, after all, been in the liberal camp himself at first. He had fought for his rights and lost. Now he said to the French ambassador, "All I want is a small corner of earth where I am master. So long as I do not have this small corner of earth I shall not be able to exercise in their fullness my spiritual functions either."

In June of 1877 Pius celebrated his golden jubilee as bishop. Cardinals, archbishops and bishops of all the former Papal States gathered in Rome to listen to Cardinal Pecci, who had been chosen to give the address of felicitation, which he had himself written. White-haired, tall and very thin, obviously an aging man, he stood before them and faced the old pope on his throne. The deep-set eyes had the old appeal, the voice its old timbre and the words he spoke were vivid and clear as his words had always been. He spoke to the pope in words of sympathy and love, and he dwelt on the great devotion of his people all over the world. His words were so eloquent, so affectionate, so understanding, that Pius was weeping when the address was ended.

All that summer there were pilgrimages in the pope's honor. An occasional protest was heard but no demonstrations occurred. Even so it was an uneasy quiet. And, as if timed, just before the celebration began, the government of Italy passed a Clerical Abuses Bill, intended to punish any priest who was heard to say anything derogatory about the government. Also there was some rude treatment of pilgrim groups, but that was soon stopped. The pilgrims spent so much money in Rome that it would have been very unwise to anger them.

Cardinal Pecci had not been well that spring and the doctor in Perugia recommended that he stay in Rome for some time. This he did, spending long happy hours with his Jesuit brother, sometimes assisting the weary old pope with audiences come to congratulate him on his jubilee. Those months had another advantage for him. He had been so long away from the papal court that now he met many dignitaries whom up to that time he had known only by hearing about them or reading their words.

He had been back in Perugia only briefly when word came that Cardinal Antonelli, who had been too ill to help much with the jubilee, had died. He was to be the last of the men who made a career of the office of secretary of state.

Not long after his death came that of Cardinal de Angelis,

the pope's chamberlain. The cardinal's death was a great
blow to the old pope, already grievously ill himself. For de
Angelis had not only been close to him and greatly loved,
but they both came from the same Adriatic shore and were
born within a month of each other. In the same month both
had been raised to the purple. Cardinal Mastai-Ferretti's vote
in the conclave following the death of Gregory XVI had been
given to de Angelis and the latter had cast his for Mastai-
Ferretti. Both had suffered for their faith, the one in exile,
the other in prison.

Not long before, Cardinal Pecci had sent out a Lenten
pastoral letter to his people, one on which he had been
working for some time, both in Rome and at Perugia. Though
no one realized it at the time, it was to be his last in the
diocese where he had been so long. In part it attacked the
liberals' opinion that the Church was hostile to the progress
of industry and science, and that there was incompatibility
between its position and civilization in its purely material
aspects. The cardinal denied this and spoke movingly of the
scientist and his role in the present day.

What the Church wanted to see come about, he wrote, was
that man should have true security and an honest recom-
pense for his labor: "Daily every man places bread to his
lips. What work to produce this! How many hands it takes
before it reaches him, from the farmer who cuts the furrow
to sow the seed to the baker who turns flour to bread. Is man
ignorant? Think of the books printed for him and the teachers provided. He needs religion and he finds men who have
given up home and pleasures to provide it. Society is indis-
pensable for our wants and so are its inventions and discoveries. Old unsafe bridges and disagreeable coach journeys
are not equals to railroads which, as it were, have fastened

wings on our shoulders and made our globe smaller, so near each other have they brought the nations.

"Vengeance and torture are no longer tolerated as man improves his relations with others and his political conditions—this is civilization.

"And whence comes this progress? Above all from labor, despised by ancient philosophers but elevated and honored by Christianity. Apostles worked, monks worked. Trade and the arts have given employment—but now danger arises. The Church does not endure it that men and women and children's health should be sacrificed to riches."

The cardinal objected to modern schools of political economy which "regard man as a machine and more or less valuable as he is more or less productive." He asked if the Church was jealous of her great men—Bacon, who said that a little knowledge leads from God but much more leads back to Him—or Copernicus or Kepler or Volta or Galileo, "whom experimental science has to thank for his powerful stimuli," or Faraday or Linnaeus. They were all men of science and men of faith as well.

"Consider the scientist," he wrote. "How majestic man appears when he seizes the thunderbolt and makes it fall powerless at his feet; when he summons the electric spark and sends it as his messenger through the abysses of ocean, across lofty mountains, over interminable plains, when he commands steam to fasten wings to his shoulders and carry him over land and sea almost with the rapidity of lightning. . . . when by ingenious processes he imprisons that force and leads it to give not only movement but intelligence, we may say, to matter which then replaces man and spares him the severest fatigues. Is there not almost a spark of his Creator in man when he summons forth the light and causes it to dissipate the darkness of night? The Church, that affectionate mother, knows all this and so far from putting obstacles in the way, she is filled with satisfaction."

He added that had he the time he would like to write a long treatise on this matter and he promised, "We shall return to this subject at some future day."

This he was to do one day with great effect, but not in Perugia. In July the pope recalled him to Rome to replace de Angelis as chamberlain.

Now that the time had come to leave, now that he was fully vindicated by being given one of the most important posts at the Vatican, he found it hard to go. He had been a vigorous young man of thirty-six when he first came, disappointed at his lost career, all but unwilling to believe his high hopes had been dashed to the ground. Now he was a man of sixty-seven, white-haired, often weary and in delicate health. That very year, in a letter to his brother in Rome, he had added a brief poem of his own which was filled with nostalgia for their happy days of childhood.

Perhaps, he thought, it was too late to change. It might be better to live out his last years among his flock who loved him and were unaffectedly sorry to lose him.

In his last talk with them he urged his people to be unafraid of the future, to face it bravely and hopefully. Even if more and more governments seemed to be in rebellion against the Church, even if socialism and its false doctrines seemed to be winning a temporary victory, he urged them to remember that this one powerful help always remained to them: "You have an invincible weapon wherewith to defend yourselves—prayer."

He reached Rome in August to meet with as fine a welcome as had been the affectionate farewell at Perugia. It was clear that many were happy to see the exile back. Before long he realized, too, that he was better informed than he had thought he would be of the trends at Rome. The people who had visited him at Perugia over the years had given him a good background on people and events at the Vatican. It was also clear that his appointment as chamberlain, coming so soon after the death of Antonelli, was strong evidence that Pius wished to show his confidence in Cardinal Pecci. And it was no easy task he had been given. To be the pope's chamberlain meant the official must "manage the property of the Church, keep up the military forces of the Holy See, be ready for war, maintain peace and have special regard for monies."

In January of 1878 King Victor Emmanuel of Italy was dying. Pius IX sent a priest to the palace to free the king from the sentence of excommunication placed on him years before. But, when the king died some days later, no church bells in Rome tolled for him. None of the hierarchy was among the mourners.

When a new king came to the throne, Pius, in one of the last acts of his life, sent a protest through Cardinal Simeoni, his secretary of state, and said firmly that he could not in any way consent to what most people by that time considered an accomplished fact—the loss of papal temporal power. He maintained the rights of the Church "to her most ancient domain" and derided the pretensions of the new king. But a few days later he said to one of the cardinals, "It is time for me to depart. Other men are needed and other methods. I know there must be a change but it must be left to my successor. I cannot break now with the tradition of my reign."

In his last years he uttered few of the pleasantries and witty remarks which had made him so delightful a companion. His bonhomie had left him. He knew his hour was

over and that the Vatican must meet new demands, but under another man than himself. There was no doubt that it
had added to the sorrow of his last years to see how empty
a place the palace was now compared to the days when he
was a young man. There were now only a few powers who
still had diplomats accredited there.

One day in 1878 Cardinal Pecci wrote to his former flock
at Perugia, "I implore you, dear brethren and most beloved
children, fervently to ask God that he will soon deign to
grant a new head to the Church and when he shall be elected
will crown him with the buckler of His virtue so that the
Bark of Peter may be safely guided through the surging
waters to the longed-for haven."

For Pius IX was dying. The stout will that had never bent
was bending at last, but only before death itself. He had
made no further statement since the one he sent the new
king on his pretended sovereignty over what was the property of the Church. He was well aware of his approaching
end. In fact, when he was told some weeks before of the
grave illness of Victor Emmanuel, he said, "The Lord knocks
at his door. If He knocks at mine I shall open to Him at
once."

On the Feast of the Purification he had taken part in the
ceremony of the distribution of candles. For the first time in
a month he had left his bed and everyone thought he looked
much better. When afterward he gave a short talk to the
parish priests of Rome, his voice was clear and firm. But next
day he slipped and almost fell. The doctors said the shock
had been too much for him and had brought about a relapse.
A few days later they said he was dying.

Beside his bed stood the cardinal Camerlingo. "Holy
Father, bless us all," he said.

Pius, his face deathly pale, said, "I bless the Sacred College and I pray God He will give them light to make a good

choice." Then he lifted the little wooden cross which contained a fragment of the True Cross. "I bless the whole Catholic world," he said.

Before long he could not speak any more but he was still conscious. Beside the dying pope stood a cardinal praying aloud. "Depart, Christian soul," he intoned and suddenly Pius managed with a great effort to speak. "Yes, yes, I depart," he said faintly, and died. About his bed gathered the Franciscan Conventuals whose privilege it was to say the prayers for the dying at every papal deathbed. Next day in every church in Rome a notice of his death was posted.

The longest rule of the papacy had ended, the years of triumph, of exile, of glory and sorrow and shattered hopes. He had known them all in his long term of office. He had been a peace-loving man but he had cut himself from the world of peace by his own proud intention. Much of his life had been a battle. He had lost on the political field but he had won more than one victory on the field of the Faith. Perhaps it was that he had been born into an unfortunate time, one when political unity had become the one word to which Italians rallied. The intellectual Mazzini, the daring Garibaldi, the political Cavour, had all been arrayed against his tenets.

Against Pius' personal character no word had ever been spoken. The only criticism had been of his stubborn resistance to a united Italy, a united Germany, a French republic. With his death an era had come to an end.

Chapter Seven

THE funeral ceremonies for the dead pope and the arrangements for the conclave which was to follow fell to a considerable degree to Cardinal Pecci in his office as papal chamberlain.

There had been apprehension at the Vatican lest the Italian government would in some way try to interfere with the various ceremonies connected with the burial of a pope. But it was soon clear that nothing untoward would take place. In fact, the government had already issued a statement that it wanted the conclave to be independent. Even so the cardinals were anxious to give the government no pretext for crossing the Vatican threshold.

Already rumors were flying about, including one from the *London Times:* the four great powers had agreed on the man who was to be the next pope. One rumor had it that there was a plot to invade the Vatican and that it had been discovered just in time. The Piedmontese government was reputed ready to seize the Vatican and also St. Peter's. Another rumor was that the great powers were unwilling to allow the cardinals to select a pope at all. There was also much speculation about the next pope but, as Cardinal Mathieu said, people always catch conclave fever—"contagious and periodic, of which science will never kill the microbe."

This was the first death of a pope since the fall of papal

power and many things would have to be carried out very differently. The custom hitherto had been to have the body lie in state in the Pauline Chapel and to admit any people who came. If the pope died in the Vatican, the body was placed in the Sistine Chapel. However, that chapel was in the Vatican itself. If the people were allowed to come there, the doors would have to be open to anyone—including the municipal police, did they choose to enter. Cardinal Pecci decided to take no chances. The body was to lie in state at St. Peter's and, in order to avoid any trouble, placed in the Blessed Sacrament Chapel, the railing before it to be closed. For the stipulated days of mourning, Masses would be said there for the soul of the dead pontiff. Pius had asked to be buried at San Lorenzo Outside the Walls, but the decision concerning that request would be made later.

Pius VIII and Gregory XVI had been elected at the Quirinal, as had Pius IX, but that palace was now the official residence of the king. In other years the cardinals had gone in state through the streets of Rome to St. Peter's where Mass was celebrated, their purple replacing the scarlet as a sign of mourning. Such a procession in 1878 would have invited possible disaster and Cardinal Pecci was taking no chances of that. What he—and in fact all the Catholic world—wanted was that the Italian government and the radical elements should find no possible cause for interfering with the conclave.

Meantime, at a preliminary meeting of the College of Cardinals—the thirty-eight who were in or close to Rome—the camerlingo produced statements he had found among Pius' papers, regulations in case of his death. There were three, the first written in 1871, the third in 1877.

The first, written just after the loss of Rome, gave the cardinals the right to elect a pope with no secular inter-

ference. If the pope was away from Rome when he died—
no doubt Pius was thinking of a possible second exile—then
this regulation would aid them. And, no matter where they
met, and if at least half the cardinals were present, the election was to be held.

The second paper was very similar, but the third went
much further, since the situation had by that time become
much more serious. This paper provided that the cardinals
could, if it were necessary, hold the conclave outside Italy.
If they had begun to vote and were in danger, they could
continue, and validly, elsewhere.

At this point Cardinal di Pietro spoke. He was very conservative, the only cardinal who still wore knee breeches
and red stockings. He said the conclave ought to be held in
Rome. He read a letter which he, as acting dean of the
Sacred College, had received from Signor Mancusi, minister
of public worship, which promised freedom and security for
the conclave. When he had finished Cardinal Simeoni said
that he felt very nervous about having the conclave meet in
Rome, but he withdrew his objection when another cardinal
pointed out that "departure would raise the problem of
returning."

A preliminary vote was taken. The result of the vote
showed twenty-two in favor of remaining in Italy, and eight
who suggested going elsewhere. Later another vote was
taken and this resulted in thirty-one voting to stay and five
to go. This was so clearly a majority vote that a date for the
conclave was set. It was to be held in the Vatican on
February 18.

Pius had left another paper, directing the camerlingo to
go at once after the pope's death to the Vatican and take

possession of the papal apartments and remain there. He was
to see that no one was admitted to the pope's rooms without
his permission. For this there was a very good reason. Some
years before, Crispi, then home secretary, as he still was, had
had a law passed that the government of Italy might enter
the pope's apartments after his death and might even enter
the conclave chamber if the supreme court allowed it. Even
though the government had now promised that all would go
well, some were uneasy about the way in which this had
been phrased. To say that the government would not interfere and at the same time promise that armed guards would
be provided if necessary was hardly a calming offer to those
who thought back to what had happened in 1870.

On the last of the days of mourning the pope's body was
brought home and placed in the Sistine Chapel. With every
cardinal in his place, a pontifical Mass was sung and in the
evening Pius IX was buried. It had been decided to hold his
funeral very quietly and at night and to place him tem-
porarily in St. Peter's, but with no elaborate funeral procession. However, word had spread through the city and the
faithful had gathered—and so had others.

As the funeral train left the Vatican many people were
following it quietly, praying as they walked along. Suddenly
mobs appeared, shouting and cursing, hurling insults at the
dead pope, throwing stones at the hearse and yelling that the
body should be thrown into the Tiber. At the head of the
funeral train walked the imperturbable camerlingo, paying no
attention to the noisy demonstrators, who made no attempt
to carry out their threats but ran off when the body had been
carried to its temporary resting place.

The new king of Italy had sent a message of condolence.

But in the funeral procession and at the services no government official had been present.

On February 18 sixty-one cardinals were in their places in the Pauline Chapel to assist at the Mass of the Holy Spirit which was to open the conclave. They had all gathered as quickly and as quietly as possible, still fearful of some unpleasant surprise on the part of the government. All but four of the screens with chair and canopy were purple. The green screens marked the places of the very old cardinals who were the only survivors of the conclave of 1846 and who had voted in the election of Pius IX.

One of the French cardinals had been very ill ever since his arrival. Two others had not arrived, Cardinal Cullen of Ireland and Cardinal McCloskey of New York, the first North American cardinal, who had been created but a few years before. It was doubtful if Cardinal McCloskey could reach Rome within the required ten days.

On all the rest the doors of the Sistine Chapel were now closed and the solemn business of electing a new pope began. With bitter irony someone had said that this would be like electing the chaplain of a cemetery.

Everything was very different from other conclaves. Earlier elections had been held in the Quirinal Palace and people had watched the imposing ceremonies which preceded the actual meeting. But there could be no meeting at the Quirinal now. Over it floated not the white and gold of the papacy but the flag of Italy with the red cross of Savoy. The Mass of the Holy Spirit was sung, not in St. Peter's and before a large public, but quietly and in the Vatican.

Even though the government had seemed to show no interest whatever in the election, Rome was buzzing with excitement. Who would be chosen? Would Austria exercise its ancient veto? Would Spain and France claim one, too? Would the foreign cardinals, such as Manning and Leda- chowski and Hohenlohe, act on their own or would they have to consider the opinions of their governments?

Manning had clearly expressed his own feelings—this was no time to elect a foreigner; what was needed was an Italian —but a good one. It was no time to rouse public feeling to a greater degree than had already been done. He had himself spoken highly of his own regard for Cardinal Pecci and said he knew people in other countries were doing the same.

The Belgian minister to the Holy See had been very vocal about the high esteem in which the archbishop of Perugia was held in the diplomatic world. But some thought that his brief time as camerlingo might militate against him, although he had corrected various abuses and seen to it that all, no matter how high in rank they were, carried out their work. There were Antonelli men among the cardinals, too, and they spoke freely of their own candidates. Cardinal Sacconi felt that Pecci was not even to be considered. He was "too modern, too averse to present policy—and too sickly." Cardinal Randi still hoped to see Martinelli elected—"a very holy Augustinian who goes out in the world as little as possible and sees few people. The pope chosen this time must be one of saintly love and very near to God."

Another cardinal who overheard this said dryly, "But he must be useful to the Church, too. Don't forget that Celestine gave up the papacy. If he hadn't the Church might have suf- fered greatly."

"And Celestine might not be canonized today," said an- other cardinal, even more dryly.

They were all united on one thing, however—a pope must be chosen and nearly all of them felt it must be done quickly.

There was need of a spokesman with authority. It was no partisan statement to say that the Church, at least where Italy was concerned, was in a sorry state. The Papal States had been absorbed into the Kingdom of Italy. There was a hostile ruler in the Quirinal. Germany and Russia had broken off diplomatic relations with the Vatican. France, its leader republican and radical, was ready to break off, too. There was no representative from England at the Vatican, though there was a cardinal—Manning. There was no diplomat from the United States, and its only cardinal was not at the conclave. As for actual property the Church had in Rome only on sufferance of the state of Italy the precarious tenure of the Vatican and its gardens. Many felt that the next pope's inheritance would be one of hopelessness.

The College of Cardinals was also, even in itself, a divided body. On one side were those who wanted no pope who would bring in a spirit of newness and modernity. Instead they wanted a man of prayer who would leave everything to the providence of God. Another group was willing to face a changing world and even help make the change. The two groups were utterly opposed to each other in their attitudes regarding modern society and the future. But they were all aware of one thing—the future must either be faced boldly or turned away from entirely.

Of the cardinals present twenty were non-Italian, enough perhaps to sway the vote if they moved in a bloc. This was considered a real danger, especially after the rumor spread that France was eager to exercise its veto and that Austria and Spain would support her.

Again and again in discussions among priests and people the name of Pecci came up. His people had loved him. He had been an able archbishop. He was highly trained in civil and canon law. When someone said he had the reputation of

being very penurious, someone else said it was a very praise-
worthy quality for a pope to have.

When the first vote was taken, Cardinal Pecci had twenty-
three votes. On the second he had thirty-eight. A third would
not be taken until the next day.

That evening Don Calensio, Cardinal Bartolini's secretary,
asked where Pecci was and his secretary said, "In the next
room. He looks like a ship in a big storm."

Calensio found Pecci sitting with his back to St. Peter's
piazza. He was very pale, even more than usual. He looked
up at the newcomer and gave a deep sigh.

"Your Eminence, why are you in such a state?" asked
Calensio.

Pecci looked at him, his dark eyes appealing. "You know
what they want of me," he said.

"Of course I know and I cannot blame you for being
troubled. We know that today Holy Church is like a yard
filled with serpents and the workers are in danger of being
bitten. But the thing to think of is that the Ship of Peter has
no pilot now. If you are asked to take the helm—what can
you do? And it is very true that no one has received so many
votes as you."

"But I am old," said Cardinal Pecci, "and I am far from
strong. If I took on this terrible burden I'd be gone in two
weeks—in less than one in all likelihood. It is not the papacy
which is being offered me. It is really—death."

Calensio smiled a little at his violence. He came up to
him and stood before him. "Eminence, what you are being
asked to take—the present state of the Church—is not your
fault nor mine either. But this I do think. I am of the firm
conviction that it is the will of God that you become pope.
I do not think it is the will of men. They are merely instru-

ments. So I do pray you that when tomorrow comes you do not refuse this which comes from God."

The slim hands clasped and unclasped as if in real despair, but Cardinal Pecci said nothing.

"Remember," said Calensio, "the day you were ordained? The promises you made then? That was a gift from God to you . . . oh, my dear Pecci, you cannot have the gift from Heaven without the bitter cup, too."

Pecci looked up. "But I had already decided to refuse," he said, almost pleadingly.

Calensio looked at him with deep compassion. "You remember it was Gregory the Great who said that renunciation of the highest honors was not always a sign of humility but often a manifestation of pride—and your conscience is clear. At no time have you intrigued for votes. Now come, Eminence, you will have to obey. And this is all there is to be said."

"But I am so old—so weak. Look at me," said Pecci.

Calensio knew that was true. "I know—I know—but I know, too, that God makes the weak strong when the need arises. And there is a need today. Trust Him and not yourself."

"I promise you it will be a very short pontificate," said Pecci. "They will have to hold another conclave at once— you'll see."

The other man smiled. "That depends on God, too. If He wants you to be pope for only a few days—well, does it matter if God wants it that way?"

Cardinal Pecci looked at the other man searchingly. "You really think there is no other way?"

"I think it is the will of God," said Don Calensio firmly.

For the first time Cardinal Pecci smiled a little. Then he answered the other's questioning look. "I was just thinking of Alexander VII when he realized he was going to be elected and what he quoted: 'Unless I am mistaken, then the day is already at hand which, bitter but an honor, you, O gods, have wanted me to have.'"

Calensio recognized the quotation from Horace and then saw a second small smile on Pecci's face. "But perhaps an invocation to pagan gods is not quite appropriate here."

At least, reflected his visitor as he left him, Pecci was in a better mood and more ready to accept. He met Cardinal Manning in the next room and spoke to him in a low voice. "I've been trying to comfort Pecci," he said, knowing well where Manning's sympathies lay.

The English cardinal nodded. "For his own sake it seems a pity that he may well be chosen. One would think a peaceful pastoral life of over thirty years would lead to eternal rest rather than to the stormy steering of Peter's Bark," he said.

Cardinal Randi was still trying to bring about a delay in the selection of successor to Pius IX. Why, he once more asked Cardinal Bartolini, were they in such a hurry for an election? At last out of patience, the latter burst out, "I shall act as my conscience tells me to. Please do not question me any more, Eminence."

By noon Cardinal Pecci had been elected. He had forty-four votes, more than were needed. He was 273 in the long line of Roman pontiffs.

"Do you accept?" asked the Cardinal Dean.

Cardinal Pecci spoke with obvious effort. "I am unworthy of this honor, but I submit to God's will."

"And what name will you assume?"

"Leo XIII, because of the gratitude I have had since my youth for Leo XII and the devotion I have had always for Leo the Great."

He had chosen a name wonderful in the Church. There
was the Leo before whom Attila withdrew, the Leo who
crowned Charlemagne and worked to unite Eastern and
Western churches, the Leo who saved Rome from the Sara-
cens, the Leo who combated clerical simony. Every one of
them was a saint in the calendar.

Several of the cardinals and his valet Baldassari helped
the pope-elect robe. His solicitous valet saw that he was
trembling and brought him a glass of wine and a little cake.

The canopies had been lowered, all but his. He gave his
benediction to the cardinals and then seated himself. The
sapphire episcopal ring was drawn from his finger and the
new Fisherman's Ring was placed there. Then Cardinal
Caterini, the chief of deacons, went to the loggia above St.
Peter's square and announced to the waiting thousands the
new pope and his name. Shouts rose from the great throng
gazing up at him, "Papa Pecci!" "Papa Pecci!" Bells pealed
from all the churches of Rome. The one thing missing was
that no cannon announced the event from Castel Sant'
Angelo's ramparts, as had been the custom in other years.

The new pope had wanted to give his first blessing from
the outside gallery, according to the ancient tradition. He
hoped in this way to show Rome his great desire to bring
peace between Church and state. When he learned that, in
this first election of a pope after the loss of temporal power,
it would be an imprudent gesture, he gave it from an opened
window in the interior loggia.

As the tall white-haired man, clad in the white cape and
stole, wearing the white biretta, stood there, the thousands
below him cheered until he stretched out his hands. Then
there was silence. He knelt for a moment in prayer, then rose
and gave his first benediction to the city and the world.

When he came back into the Vatican he was smiling but his face looked drawn. It was evident that he was very tired. Yet he had a look of peace. It was as if now, with his mind made up, he was ready for work. Years before, when he had met with the bitter disappointment of seeing the diplomatic career, which he had hoped for and been trained for, seemingly vanish forever, he had written, "What hopes can I have of victory? I prefer to put away such disturbing thoughts and place my confidence in God who began the task and Who alone can bring it to an end. I have no hope but in Him." He could have repeated that now.

On the day of his election he wrote only one letter, and that to his family: "Dearest brothers, I must tell you that by this morning's ballot the Sacred College has raised me to St. Peter's Chair. This is my first letter. I send you my apostolic blessing and with all my love. Pray for me fervently to God.　　pp Leo XIII."

During the next days he wrote the customary letters to temporal rulers and heads of state. They were similar but each had a personal note. Each mentioned the hope of a better future. They were to go to Victoria of England, the president of the United States, the emperor of Austria, the kings of the Netherlands and Sweden, of Norway and Denmark, the czar of Russia, the president of Switzerland, the emperor of Germany.

He wrote them with great care and went over the wording several times. Some of the cardinals offered to help him. The new pope thanked them, but this he felt was something that he must handle himself, so that it would be personal as well as official. The one government to which went no official announcement of his election was his own Italy. The government, on its part, paid no attention whatever to the fact that a new pope had been elected.

At Perugia it was very different. Bells were rung and houses were lighted and bonfires blazed when the news reached the city. Next day in every church there was a solemn Mass of thanksgiving and many prayers that God would guide their cardinal through the storms and darkness of the years ahead.

Chapter Eight

SEVERAL days after his election Pope Leo came to his private study, where already a great pile of letters and papers lay on the wide desk, some addressed to his predecessor, some already come for him. One letter among those addressed to him caught his attention and, quite by chance, he opened it first of all. It proved so unusual that he read it through with a deepening interest. The writer said he was a member of the Saint-Simon Society and that he had been deeply interested over the years in Cardinal Pecci's statements on science and also on the social order.

The pope was well aware of the identity of Saint-Simon as well as of his theories. As a young man Saint-Simon had fought on the side of the American colonies and had returned to engage in the revolution at home. In later years he had put his considerable fortune to helping develop his social theories which were, basically, that the forces which control society and are now in the hands of scientists and industrialists must be used to bring about a better world order and not used selfishly for personal or national gain. He had written a book—*The New Christianity*—to explain his belief that science and industry must be affiliated with the brotherhood of man.

It was also very true that since his death in 1825 his ideas had become so altered that his followers were, to most students of the social scene, practically socialists. All this the present writer to the Holy Father admitted, but he added that hitherto the Church and scientific developments were, in the eyes of many, hostile to each other. He was writing because of a hope that the pope would remember that the theories of Saint-Simon were basically Christian, as indeed Saint-Simon himself had been a Catholic.

In earlier days, the letter went on, the Church had been the place to which the poor and oppressed came for protection. Surely then the Church should give protection to the working classes of today whom industrialism was oppressing. If the pope—and the writer was aware that His Holiness had a deep interest in this phase of present-day life—would use his great talents in his high place the writer felt sure that a new social order would come through his efforts.

It was a strange letter to open as one of the first of the many messages on his desk. What the writer had said was of course very true, for, as monsignor and bishop and arch-bishop and cardinal, Leo had observed in other countries this development of industry, which had come somewhat later and in lesser degree to Italy. He had known of tremendous fortunes made by the few at the expense of the many. He had seen men hungry and sometimes homeless because there was so small a wage given them—if, in fact, there was any work at all for them.

He sat with the letter in his hand and pondered. Marx was strongly influencing these abused people and calling for a classless society and a battle to be continued until the proletariat won the world. Against Marx was balanced in Leo's mind Thomas Aquinas, who wrote on the divine order in the world as assigned by God. The world needed change, on that point Marx was right, but surely there need not be chaos to achieve that change. The world must come back to this order ordained by God. Marx was right, too, in saying that it was in the working classes that the strongest power was being formed. But that did not mean that such power could not be used for the purposes of God if only people could be made to understand where their material and spiritual hope of a good future lay.

Leo laid the letter down. What had interested him especially about it was that already he had, as pope, come to a decision. In a way this letter was confirming him in it by asking him to do the one thing he had already planned to do—bring Catholic action into the very center of the stirring world of workers. He would prove that divine Love is greater than human selfishness and hate.

Leo had hoped that his coronation might take place in St. Peter's. In fact, preparation had begun for that. The grand tapestries from the Vatican were being hung along the nave when the order came to stop the work. At first Leo was amazed. He had been too long away to realize how strongly revolutionary ideas and violence filled the city. Even despite the mob violence he had witnessed only recently he had thought a coronation ceremony in St. Peter's immune to such action. It was when he learned that the city government was refusing to take any precautions to maintain order during the ceremony that he agreed to have the services in the Sistine Chapel. In fact he began to understand even more what Pius IX had meant when he said, "It becomes more and more understood by more and more people that one can live in Rome as pope only by remaining a prisoner in the Vatican."

However, the coronation was to take place with all its past formality, with a colorful procession going from the

papal apartments to the Pauline Chapel, through the Scala
Regia to the Sistine Chapel. Not one iota of the time-honored
ceremonial was to be omitted.

Already, during the days since his election, the pope had
received many people, among them the diplomatic corps
and dignitaries from near and far who were flocking to Rome
for the occasion. The audiences lasted for as much as nine
hours and in one day he spoke to a thousand people, each of
whom came separately to kneel and receive his blessing.
Once his attendants urged him to stop for that day, but he
looked at the people waiting in the throne room and thought
of the others waiting to enter.

"No, no," he said. "All these people have come from so far.
We must see them. If I see one I must see them all." And he
was happy that he had made the decision when he learned
that one group waiting was a delegation from his own
Perugia.

On the day of the coronation the Sistine Chapel saw the
glittering array of other days. In the royal box were the Duke
and Duchess of Parma. Every cardinal was present. Prince
Colonna was there in the picturesque costume of the time of
Philip II. There were mitered abbots, the Order of St. John of
Jerusalem, Knights of Calatrava and others. Wearing their
decorations and medals were the ambassadors and ministers
still accredited to the Vatican. One box held a score of ladies
in black dresses and long lace mantillas.

The pope in scarlet mozzetta was carried on his sedia from
the Pauline Chapel, with a full court and an escort of nobles
and Swiss guards. Between slowly moving fans of ostrich
plumes he moved along, silver trumpets heralding his arrival.
He wore a white cape, embroidered white gloves, a white-
and-gold miter.

When he descended from the sedia before the altar the

Mass began. After the Confiteor he sat on his throne while the Cardinal Deacon removed his miter and another cardinal placed on his shoulders the pontifical pallium. Then he received the obedience of the cardinals and proceeded to the altar to continue the Mass.

After it was finished a tiara was placed on his head. "Receive the tiara with three crowns," said Cardinal Mertel as he set it in place. Leo had chosen the one given to Pius IX by the Palatine Guard of Honor. He seemed very frail to be wearing so heavy a burden, but he gave no evidence of weakness. After the benediction had been given all present, he was borne from the chapel.

Later, in the Hall of Tapestries, with all the cardinals about him, he listened to Cardinal di Pietro read an address to him. He answered briefly and when he spoke of the weight of the Keys—"of itself so formidable"—and of the solemnity of the ceremony just ended, there was for the first time a touch of weariness and almost of fear in his voice. Very slowly he repeated King David's words: " 'Who am I, O Lord, that Thou hast brought me here,' " and then he sighed deeply. He looked at the assembled cardinals as if for some comfort and added that it was true that God sometimes chose the weak to confound the strong—"so we hope He will sustain us in our weakness to make glowing His strength."

More than one of those who had been close to him since his election breathed a sigh of relief that he had lived at least for his coronation. The Marquis de Vogüé, who had been one of those to attend him, said it had seemed to him like the "exaltation of a ghost."

The church bells rang in Rome in the new pope's honor and that night in the time-honored fashion many palaces and houses were brightly lighted. Within an hour street gangs like those which had desecrated Pius' funeral train gathered and began smashing every window where a light showed, shouting threats and cursing.

It had been very different at Perugia, Leo learned. There bells rang and homes were lighted and remained so. Bonfires blazed as on the day his election had been announced. He was happy when he was told of that.

Perhaps one of the best tributes came to the new pope from England. When the news of the near riot which followed his coronation was learned there, Cardinal Manning said, "The world can take nothing from him and from the world he asks nothing but the obedience of faith ... His power is not of this world yet it is world-wide and it is dependent on God alone ... The successor of Peter walks erect on the water for his faith never falters and his Master holds him by the hand."

There were many things to try him during his first days as pope—small, unhappy things, as when the mayor and the council of Rome renamed many of the streets with names of anticlericals and set up a revolving light with the red, white and green of Savoy, which was turned on each evening on the summit of the Janiculum Hill just opposite the Vatican.

Despite the many fears expressed concerning him, Leo continued to remain alive. More than that, he continued working. Wrote one visiting bishop, almost in awe, "This old man, one would think, would be looking into the past, but he has his eyes on the future. He enters resolutely on this path with amazing clairvoyance. Believers see in this the effect of a higher aid; nonbelievers see the work of genius. Either explanation sets an aureole about his head."

Leo had taken on, as one of his first tasks, the reconstruction of the hierarchy of Scotland, a cherished project of Pius IX, which his death left uncompleted. It was now fully restored. The ancient see of St. Andrew—"recalled now from the tomb," wrote Leo—was to be the See of Edinburgh. Glasgow, too, was to be made into an episcopal see.

"It is a happy omen," wrote Leo, "with which to begin the exercise of the Supreme Pastorate which we have taken on ourselves with fear and trembling amid the calamities of modern times," and he ended by asking as intercessors for Scotland its beloved St. Andrew and also Blessed Margaret, once queen of that land—"to bless this church born again."

He took occasion to point out that Catholics were greatly increasing in Scotland and mentioned also the great progress Catholicism had made in England since 1850. In September of that year he intended to create in England the See of Leeds.

It did not take long to see that those long years of exile from Rome for which Antonelli had been in the main responsible had produced a planning ability which was now ready to be shared and put to practical use. It was also soon clear that the Vatican was going to have to recognize the modern world and live with it. National unities were becoming realities, as were colonial empires. Democracies were on the rise, and the forces of revolution were in ferment.

Earlier popes had refused to have the palace lighted with gas. The new pope was not afraid of it. As archbishop of Perugia he had written a pastoral in which he spoke of Galileo as one whom "experimental science has to thank for its powerful stimuli." He spoke admiringly of modern science as "the high stage of glory which man has now reached" and he did not fear the enlightening even when he condemned the Enlightenment in many ways. "It is best," he said one day, "in certain cases to leave metaphysics and come down to the practice of the concrete."

The Antonelli opposition, still very much alive, soon saw that what they had feared would happen was already coming to pass. This was a very different man from the often explosive and often opinionated Pius. Gambetta was soon calling him, with studied insult, elegant and subtle, a diplomat rather than a priest, and versed in every intrigue. He thought this new pope would die soon, but "if not, we may expect a marriage of convenience between the Church and the modern state."

He was right in that there would be activity on the part of the new pope who was, it soon became clear, ready to attack, but as ready to make terms, granted only that the eternal values of the Church were not injured. Basically his progress was very concrete. It was also shattering to some at the Vatican who were little by little seeing the shape of things to come and who could hardly believe the change. Pius IX had almost categorically refused to reconcile himself with modern progress, whereas Leo XIII spoke of the great progress of modern times—"to aid the well-being of the body and material things. All these things were given by God to help mankind. What is necessary is that all—art, science, trade, true liberty—all must be honestly used for all mankind."

Leo XIII wanted three things for the future and from the beginning of his reign he spoke often and in many ways of these—to bring society back to the Gospel, not merely in philosophical talk among theologians, but in action; to bring back good relations as much as possible with secular powers; and to create no useless difficulties for the new government of Italy, though he insisted it must always be emphasized that the papacy was the glory of the country and that to it Italy owed everything of value in the past. In his first consistorial allocution he spoke of the work ahead and said he

would draw back from none of it because of fatigue. He
wanted the cardinals to share the work with him and made it
clear he would consult them often. They were, he said, like
the fifty elders of Israel whom Moses chose at God's command to help him.

Older and conservative cardinals who had been apprehen-
sive of his social-action tendencies saw whither this new
regime was tending and many were reassured to some extent. Leo was obviously determined to see that the workers
were fairly treated, as much as lay in his power to bring
about. They remembered his pastoral letter of some ten years
ago when he spoke of "colossal abuses against the poor and
weak . . . the existence to which children in factories are condemned . . . the need to pass laws which would put an end
to this inhuman traffic." The pastoral letters from Perugia
had of course been studied and with care by the Italians and
it had been made abundantly clear how interested he was in
modern society. Then, too, the intellectuals at Rome had
been fascinated by his deep knowledge of the classics and of
antiquity. Rome had not for a long time had a pope who had
such familiarity with both classic and contemporary affairs.

For his secretary of state Leo chose Cardinal Franchi,
Roman born, an able diplomat, extremely well educated, a
former envoy to Spain and Constantinople. He knew, it was
said, at least four-fifths of the bishops of the world. He had
been in Ireland several times, the last at the recent anniversary celebration of O'Connell. He knew England well,
too. He was aware that the world was changing and he did
not ignore the problems this brought but he did not think
the papacy should remain aloof from this new society. He
had been heard to say that it was one thing to condemn
separation of Church and state but quite another to separate
Church and society. Another common interest with Leo was

his great desire to help the churches in eastern Europe and also to secure a peace with Berlin.

In April Leo issued his inaugural encyclical *Inscrutabili Dei Consilio,* a very brief paper. He spoke of the contemporary evils troubling the world, the dissensions within and among nations, materialism. He spoke sadly of the rejection of the authority of the Church which was a promoter of true progress and civilization. He appealed to rulers as well as to the hierarchy and to the faithful to help in restoring religion and morality to the world.

The encyclical was in no sense argumentative. It was merely a statement of what was wrong and an expression of hopes of making things right. It was what he had been saying to the Umbrians for years and now he was saying it to the world. It had proved something of a disappointment to Italy's radicals who had expected he would immediately try to make a sort of peace with King Humbert and his regime. Instead this was a sober review of facts. There was little they could laugh at or tear to pieces. It was a statement of the sinful ways of modern society. Leo talked as if he were exactly what the conservatives had wanted, a praying pope.

The second encyclical—*Quod Apostolici muneris*—issued later in the same year, was more definite. It had as its text a verse from Isaiah: Cry out, cease not to lift your voice like a trumpet. It was an indictment of socialism and of communism, which denies all authority, seeks to destroy marriage and the family, and wants an end to private property. "The keen longing after happiness has been narrowed to the range of the present life," he wrote. "With such doctrines it is no wonder that men of the most lowly condition should fix eager eyes on the homes and fortunes of the wealthy," but he made it clear that selfish wealth and extravagant luxury were partly to blame.

He outlined the socialists' tenets and then gave the chief tenets of Catholic doctrine. Against socialism he declared war. He also spoke disparagingly of the rising sect of Christian Science as "exploiting even the Gospels the better to deceive the unwary." The tenets he condemned could be resolved to one: God is nothing. The true Christian's was: God is everything.

In the two short encyclicals he had stated what was wrong and how to right it. It was also clear that both were intended to show the world the path he meant to follow as pope. The second letter, as a matter of fact, caused some alarm among the more conservative Catholics. "Let sleeping dogs lie," was their motto. To them the social problem of which he had spoken was one of no great importance but they feared such utterances might well make it one.

He was amused when he learned of this criticism. "Those people are too old for me," he said.

Leo XIII had never lost, and would never lose, a certain delight in grandeur, inherited no doubt from the long-ago days of formality at Carpineto. His new office brought him opportunities to exercise such grandeur and there was no doubt that he relished them. He delighted in giving his blessing from the great chair in the basilica, in seeing the mass of faces lifted to him. He liked his audiences carried out with full dignity and his own attitude toward those who came to him was always gracious. He was the good host, even at audiences, and one of his deep regrets was that they were sometimes so large he could not speak an individual word to each one present.

The large audiences were, however, extremely formal. He

was announced by the entrance of soldiers, by the blowing of trumpets, by the staccato commands of officers. People said delightedly that he had restored the ancient sense of grandeur to the papacy.

On the other hand, he was not rigid in demands for undue formality. For instance, he once again permitted the clergy to ride bicycles, a thing which had been considered undignified for them and forbidden under the previous administration.

He liked the pomp and the trappings of his office but there was one thing of which he was unaware: the wonderful picture he himself made, especially in the great chair that seemed much too large for him when they carried him in procession down the aisle of St. Peter's. The transparently thin hand with the ring that always seemed to weigh it down when he was blessing the crowds, the beautifully proportioned head, the firmly set mouth, the sweet smile which contradicted it—"a man on the search," someone said of him. He was old in years but still young in impulse. Sometimes when he walked it was noted that he slumped and bent more than usual. But suddenly he would straighten like an arrow as if himself aware of it.

Always he carried with him, and was aware of, the special dignity of the papacy. He seldom laughed though his smile came often. And at least one quality of his predecessor was lacking in him—he rarely indulged in witty remarks.

It was soon realized that he did almost nothing without consulting the Sacred College. He showed them everything he wrote and frequently, at their suggestions, made changes. It amazed some of them to see the great amount of writing he did. "Where do you find the time, Your Holiness?" someone asked him.

He smiled. "I sleep badly. So I write."

His private life was as simple as it had always been. His

rooms were few and plainly furnished. He ate as little now as he had at Perugia. He ate alone, according to a tradition which he observed, though begun by a pope many centuries before. However, the story was told that he wanted his secretary to eat with him so that they need waste no time discussing matters together. The result was that they sat together at table, Leo eating first and then his secretary.

At his first dinner in his own papal dining room he was surprised to see the unusual number of dishes presented to him and served by Baldassari. "But why so many?" he asked. "You know what I like for dinner."

"It is I who told the cook to prepare them," said his valet. "Since Your Eminence has become pope it seems more fitting."

Leo looked at him with an amused smile. "But, Baldassari, my stomach has not become papal!"

He often rose at four in the morning. After two private Masses and a breakfast of hot chocolate or *café au lait*, he talked with his secretary, held receptions and audiences. Once when a noted Protestant was coming for an audience, his major domo came to ask the pope how he was to be received.

"Just as if he were being received by the president of the United States," Leo told him.

His simple noon meal was soup, eggs, salad, a little wine. Then, after a short nap, or perhaps only a rest in his chair, he took a drive in the gardens and usually a short walk.

"He is walking very fast today," said one monsignor, observing him.

"Oh, he was told that there is a rumor in Rome that he is ill," said another.

In the gardens was a grotto with a statue of Our Lady of Lourdes, where he went often to say his rosary. "You choose this so often rather than other spots in the gardens. You must have a deep devotion to that shrine," said someone.

"It is my bit of France," he said simply.

After the walk he would read newspapers, write letters and work on encyclicals, and then eat a simple supper. More writing followed, sometimes verse, and usually a little reading of Dante and Horace.

He liked to have news brought to him as soon as it came, even if it was late at night. "I'm sure to be awake," he said.

He had always liked seeing his close relatives and he still did. Many of them were dead now—his parents, his sisters, several of his brothers. But Giuseppe, always the closest to him of all, was still living—was, in fact, now a cardinal. It was a title he had not wanted and still did not care about. He had accepted it only because Vincenzo asked him not to refuse it.

Several times a week Giuseppe came to spend a few evening hours with his brother and they both enjoyed these meetings. They talked not so much of matters of the Church, but rather of the telephone and photography and electricity and even of the new cinematograph. Sometimes the younger brother accused the older of being still a little old-fashioned regarding these new inventions. The cardinal never stayed late for both of them had work to do before they slept. When he left the pope always went to the door with him to say good-by, as was his invariable custom with all private visitors.

Leo had always enjoyed taking long walks alone. No doubt he liked to walk alone still, even in the enclosed space of the Vatican gardens where no path led to the freedom of a wider world; where for years another pope, likewise imprisoned, had ridden his white mule along these paths.

Once Leo was heard to say he was sorry there was no opportunity to hunt in the Vatican gardens. It had been a favorite sport of earlier days. Instead he had a small private zoo, the inmates brought him by visitors, and it included a snow-white deer, a white peacock, two ostriches, a pelican and for a time a parakeet which French admirers had given him. But one day while he was taking a walk he heard a loud "Vive le Pape." It was the parakeet, trained secretly, perhaps, by someone, and the pope ordered that part of his zoo removed. "The accent was no doubt too Bourbon," quipped someone.

Leo had accepted the terms under which his predecessor had lived and remained a voluntary prisoner in the Vatican. But there was little doubt that he thought often of Carpineto, not far away, and regretted the fact that he could no longer go there. As priest, monsignor, bishop, he had gone back now and then. As pope he could not. The lack of all pageantry there had always made him happy. So had his own small room on the third floor of the palace, from whose windows he could see the street and the mountains, the old Franciscan monastery with the hills behind it and framing it. The room was as it had been many years ago when he was a boy, the same bed with its canopy, the desk, the chairs.

While he was there he said Mass in the family chapel and then went to sit in the old garden, often on the wide rim of the big stone cistern, gray with age, but with the arms of the Peccis faintly visible on its side. The trees were still there from which he had helped his mother shake fruit. There he had later read his breviary and worked on his papers and talked with his relatives. Evenings he went to the village square to chat with old friends who called him, after he had received a high title, The Eminentissimo. He told them about Rome and Perugia and Brussels and then went back to the palace to work on papers until late.

After he became pope one old man from Carpineto used to come to see him one day every year, even when the visitor was almost a hundred years old. He and Vincenzo had hunted together as boys. "You remember that quail you missed?" he asked on one occasion. The pope nodded his head ruefully.

He always welcomed this visitor with delight and talked with him of boyhood days. The old man stayed so long that monsignori grew impatient, for they had important matters to discuss. Cardinals stamped out, the business about which they had come left undone when they went.

But, when the door at last opened and Leo stood saying a gay farewell to the bent old man in his best country clothes, no one envied the hard-working pope this one day of happy memories.

People had, he was told, sometimes expressed a desire to walk with him in the garden. So, when he did not ride out in his little carriage with a monsignor of his household beside him, he often walked with guests. When he walked alone he usually read reports.

As for his dress, it was only for the great occasions which demanded it that he wore fine regalia. His love of pomp extended to the office and not to himself. Even his pectoral cross and ring he put on only when he was receiving visitors.

He had always loved flowers and in Perugia had been known as a considerable horticulturist. He had a theory that priests who lived outside the cities should get interested in the growing of flowers and fruits as an avocation. He had practiced what he preached and he tried this to a certain degree in the Vatican gardens, very much to the annoyance of the old head gardener. The gardener had been there all during the reign of Pius IX and had never once met with advice from him or even suggestions about new specimens. To a sympathetic cardinal he complained, "I'm good for nothing around here these days. The Holy Father keeps coming around and he wants to know about everything— even how I work and what I plant."

The Vatican household had soon learned that this was a very different man from the former pope and not only in his attitude toward flower beds and grapevines. Leo was not explosive but he was very highly strung. The household grew to know his days of elation, his days of depression. They grew accustomed to seeing him in silent prayer in his chapel for as much as an hour at a time, the erect figure motionless. After a while they stopped worrying about the possibility of his falling over and hurting himself. Sleep was treated as a necessary evil. He rose early and sat up late, spending an hour or two over Dante or working at his own verses in Latin. It was a great worry to his valet that he sat up so late at his writing desk, for sometimes he fell asleep there and the desk was lighted by two tall candles.

One of the new pope's worries was the fact that there was very little actual money in the Vatican treasury when he came to the papacy. It had of course been in a flourishing condition before the annexation. The years following 1848 had taken much of its funds. When Pius IX returned from exile he had lost two thirds of his states and the money which went with them. A few remained, but there also remained a large debt to be paid with interest. Then came the final take-over of Rome, its palaces and properties, so long the possessions of the Holy See.

During those years the faithful all over the world helped, in large part through the annual Peter's Pence collection. This had been suppressed during Elizabeth's reign but had been restored. With that sum the necessities of the Holy

See were met during those difficult years. There were many
expenses—the dependents, the workmen, the household,
printing and mailing, a thousand lesser items. "No government in the world conducts so large and widespread a business on so small an expenditure as the government of the
Holy Catholic Church," said Cardinal Vaughan admiringly.

During the first year of Leo's reign Cardinal Franchi died
suddenly of a heart attack and Leo was faced with the need
of finding another and like-minded ally. He finally chose
Cardinal Nina, who was very different from Franchi but,
like him, able and ready to meet the world and not withdraw
from it. Like Leo, he was willing to extend an occasional
olive branch to the Italian state, a method very different from
the continuous open hostility of Pius IX. Of course, everyone knew that Crispi could if he wished order his soldiers
to occupy the Vatican and send the pope and his household across the frontier. But no further steps were taken, no
doubt because the eyes of the world were watching.

The pilgrimages, too, continued with perfect freedom and
were never interfered with in the slightest degree. During
Leo's first year as pope a group of German pilgrims came to
the Vatican and in the next month a large group from Spain.
In the following year came a pilgrimage of Catholic writers
and journalists from many countries. As one cardinal said,
this was a very fitting group to visit Leo, for after all, the
many Perugian pastorals had made the pope something of a
journalist himself and his fine poems put him in the class of
writers. Only later it was learned that he was at the time also
writing for a Roman magazine, *Vox Urbis*, which was printed
entirely in Latin. To the column headed *Aenigmata*—that
is, the puzzle department—he contributed many unsigned
charades.

He talked with the visiting writers about books and told them he was issuing a new code of regulations for the Vatican library and that he hoped before long to open the archives for the use of writers of all faiths. He said he thought much of the sad state of present affairs in the world was due in part to a poor press. Controversy was featured rather than news.

He was himself an excellent writer of letters. Those he sent soon after his election to various rulers had brought a good response. To the emperor of Germany he had written, "To our sorrow the relations between Your Majesty and the Holy See are broken. . . . We appeal for a restoration for the peace of conscience of your Catholic subjects." To Russia had gone a very similar letter. Both touched on sore points but the letters were cordial and brought equally cordial replies.

One letter which congratulated him on his election was answered warmly and quickly—that from Père Olivaint of Paris, whom he knew well, and who was founder and president of the Society for the Encouragement and Protection of Young Artisans. During the Paris Commune he had been expelled with his followers, but they continued to work in secret throughout the land.

Another letter which was warmly answered was that from Prince de Chimay, a nobleman who devoted himself to promoting societies for workingmen in Belgium. One very warm answer went to a letter sent by the mayor and municipal council of Cork, Ireland: "We express to you our gratitude and affection. We pray God to be ever your protector and helper, my beloved sons."

In the spring of 1879 Leo filled vacancies in the ranks of the cardinals. One of the newly chosen was from England—Dr. John Henry Newman, who had entered the Church in

1845 and of whose elevation to the cardinalate Lord Palmerston, then prime minister, said it was one of the most important events in England since the Reformation.

In 1850 Pius IX had created Bishop Wiseman cardinal. When the news was made known in England, there were shouts of "No Popery" in London streets, and "Down with the Papists!" Now, some thirty years later, in that same city, a large and undisturbed meeting was held in honor of Cardinal Newman when he returned from Rome after receiving the red hat.

Chapter Nine

AUGUST OF 1879 saw the issuance of the first encyclical in which Leo turned to a subject dear to his heart for many years—the importance to the modern world of the teachings of Thomas Aquinas and, as the most practical way of promoting the science of Christian teaching, the basing of the present study of theology and philosophy on his works.

Many people, both friends and enemies, were surprised by *Aeterni Patris*. The first two brief encyclicals, the one a setting forth of what was wrong with the world, the other an exposition of Christian principles to combat this, had been an appeal to rulers and hierarchy to help. People had expected the next one to be controversial. Instead it was gentle and scholarly. It was of course rather unusual to have eight thousand words devoted almost entirely to praise of Thomas Aquinas who was by no means required reading for the intellectuals of the day—a philosopher six hundred years dead, long entombed in dusty libraries, consulted by scholars when they wanted to prove some theological point but not by the busy men of the present.

To Leo, who had read and studied him deeply during the long years at Perugia, the Angelic Doctor spoke everlasting and unvarying Catholic truth and the pope wanted everyone to know him. He had studied him so thoroughly that he

wished to have him become popular reading, not gathering
dust in unopened books and manuscripts. Since the present
world was so anxious to throw off the old which it considered
no longer useful and study only the new, he saw here an
opportunity to make known one who could bring the old to
the new and show that by following his precepts people
could live at peace in the new and also with the old. Thomas
was no pet of scholastics of course, nor was he studied by
Marxians who were anxious to overthrow, not to develop.
Leo wanted to see Thomas' great arguments used again to
appeal to those who were anxious to see an adjusted world.
Far from the ferment of Rome Cardinal Pecci had watched
and pondered a cure. To the great philosopher of long ago
the modern pope turned, invoking his aid for an ailing world.

To this decision he had come slowly but surely. He knew
that, even though older men at Rome often denied it, in order
to bring about a better understanding of the rights of both
Church and state there must be changes on the part of the
Church. When in 1867 Marx had published his *Das Kapital*,
he had said very plainly that there must be a change in the
social order. But any fundamental agreement on method
failed when Marx spoke of a material world only. He had
cited the terrible misery of the many poor and the increasing
wealth of the few rich. He said this would one day result in
the workingman's becoming the leader of a classless society.
But such a goal meant hatred of class for class, one against
the other, on the one side the exploiters, on the other the
world's dispossessed. Marx said there must be constant warfare until the proletariat won.

The working people were being won over to the belief
that the Church gave them little thought. It was time, therefore, before it was too late, for the Church to make clear that
this was not true.

Leo could not and would not admit that materialism and

antagonism were the proper answers, but he did know that there must be a quieting of hatreds between the Church and the newly rising states. Gregory XVI and Pius IX had spoken in bitter terms of the Enlightenment but neither had offered anything to take its place. It set reason above faith, of course, but reason, too, had its rights and it was certain that a man did not grow less religious because he made use of his God-given faculty of reason. Thomas Aquinas, who had read and absorbed the philosophy of Aristotle, had hoped to keep the Church from growing hostile to all development and to the use of reason. Reason to him was not enough to show a man the truth but it was an aid and not an enemy of faith, if honestly and intelligently applied.

"Faith presupposes reason," said Thomas Aquinas long ago. The new pope was to repeat and continue to repeat his words. In this, his first important encyclical, and in all future letters, the one glowing fact stood out—reason must always be complemented by the truths of faith. They must be not enemies but allies.

"Every word of wisdom," ended *Aeterni Patris*, "every useful thing by whomsoever planned or discovered, should be received with a willing mind—this we hold. We exhort you to restore the golden wisdom of Saint Thomas and to spread it for the defense and the beauty of the Catholic faith, for the good of society and for the aid of all the sciences, so that it may be as widely known as possible."

For years Aquinas had been read as a part of any good scholastic education by scholars, and then returned to his shelf. Now it was hoped he would be read and practiced. Leo went about fulfilling this hope in a very practical manner. He ordered—and himself donated the large sum of money necessary for the purpose—a new edition of St. Thomas' complete works, one which would be as accurate as possible, and he appointed a group of scholars to prepare it. He was already planning an Academy of St. Thomas at Rome and was setting up departments of scholastic philosophy at various universities. He put his great hope very clearly—that all this effort would eventually show that reason and faith could work in harmony.

He quoted Cajetan on Aquinas: "He has a sovereign veneration for all the ancient doctors and he seems to have united in himself the intellectual powers of them all." He was also, added Leo, "learned, quick-witted, a lover of truth. Singlehanded he succeeded in combating the erroneous systems of past ages and supplied weapons to the champions of truth against the errors which have and will crop out to the end of time." And he reminded his readers that at the Council of Trent the *Summa* was placed on the altar beside the Gospels—"as the most perfect and scientific exposition of revealed truth."

In his desire to put higher education on the best footing possible Leo did not, however, neglect the secondary and primary education of Roman children whose schooling now was in lay hands. In 1879 he built—and from his private funds—twenty-nine new Catholic schools and made them so good that the government schools lost many pupils. In other parts of Italy, spurred by his example, the bishops set up new schools.

Leo XIII was now facing one fact which Pius IX had refused to face—something must be done about the long-existing enmity between the Holy See and nearly all the temporal powers. There had of course been conflicts often over the centuries, but in earlier days the papacy had its lands and palaces, its armies. In the name of her Founder the Church had often claimed a supremacy over temporal and passing rulers. But those were the days when popes sometimes insisted they had the right to depose even temporal monarchs. It was also true that over the centuries more than one ruler had refused to give in, just as it was also true that Henry IV had gone to Canossa to ask that the ban of excommunication be lifted.

The last few popes had found it all but impossible to realize that those times were now gone. Pius IX and his group would not—perhaps could not—admit they were actually gone, that when Bismarck said he would never go to Canossa in body or spirit he meant exactly that. But some of the more thoughtful men in the Church were beginning to wonder how matters might have worked out if Leo had been pope when Bismarck began the long bitter fight between his government and the Church of Rome.

When Leo came to the throne matters were still very tense. One of his first efforts was to inform the people exactly what were the rights of the state and what were the rights of the Church. These first efforts produced tentative results, first on the part of Germany. In December of 1883 the prince imperial of Germany called at the Vatican and remained for an hour. Prussian radicals immediately said this was a second Canossa pilgrimage, but many people in Germany were very tired of hearing about Canossa and noted only that the pope was being moderate and patient.

By 1885 conditions had so improved that the kaiser asked Leo to arbitrate in a dispute between Germany and Spain regarding the possession of the Caroline Islands in the South Seas. Germany had taken over these islands which Spain had claimed as her own. Now a dangerous situation had developed as to who had rights to them. Leo said he could not arbitrate but he was willing to act as mediator. The plan he evolved was an agreement which recognized the prior right of Spain but gave Germany protection for its subjects living there and also commercial concessions. It was signed by both sides and was considered a real victory for diplomacy. As thanks the kaiser sent the pope a beautiful pectoral cross and in courteous return Leo bestowed on the kaiser and his chancellor honorary decorations. In statements that year he made it clear that in anything which concerned religion the Church was above the temporal state, but he made it equally clear that she could not interfere with secular laws. As he said, freedom often brought forward excellent claims but he warned it must always act within the framework of the good of the whole. Freedom which was merely the pleasure of individuals was not freedom.

These statements had a calming effect on the German government which had not been happy to hear Bismarck called a second Nero and a modern Attila by Pius IX nor to hear the persecution of Catholics in Germany referred to as a new Diocletian persecution.

The unhappy German situation had been still unchanged when Leo became pope. The Kulturkampf was still going on. During those years the Jesuits had been exiled from Germany. Bishops and priests had been expelled or imprisoned. No papal letter could be read in the churches. The seminarians had to attend the state universities. The state claimed the right to depose even bishops. The basic threat, of course, was that the Church in Germany must become a state church or perish.

Even in 1879 the situation was somewhat changed, thanks in great part to a strong Catholic Center party in the Reichstag and to Leo's prudent and conciliatory methods. In 1882 Kaiser Wilhelm I announced that diplomatic relations between Berlin and the Holy See would be resumed. Bismarck was loud in his praise of the modern and wise new pope. Bishops, long in exile, began to return to their sees. When a few years later the kaiser was celebrating his ninetieth birthday there was present at the gala banquet Monsignor Galimberti, official representative of the pope—the first time an envoy of the Holy See graced a Prussian royal table. By that time the banished religious orders had returned to Germany and Catholic schools and seminaries had reopened. In 1886 a new religious law was passed in the Prussian parliament canceling all anti-Catholic legislation and it was signed by the kaiser. This was a real triumph for the diplomacy of Leo. As for Bismarck, he had said, even before matters were thus settled, "It is brave to fight when we must but no sensible man wants to make fighting a permanent way of life."

England, too, saw fences mended. There conditions in Ireland made for trouble. The agrarian difficulties involved the rights of the peasants against tyrannical landlords as well as the burning question of Home Rule, so that there were really two great quarrels going on at the same time. The agrarian trouble was perhaps worse at the time and needed attention from the Holy See for this was a Catholic country which had for a long time suffered and been treated badly. Leo felt that the Irish were heading for violent reprisals and he wanted none of that. To him and his advisers at the Vatican there seemed danger of, in that case, rebellion against the law. He issued a warning to the Irish people which was immediately acclaimed by conservatives and landlords. It was an error to have sent that warning but it took time for the Vatican to realize that the Irish action was not a revolt but a strike against intolerable conditions. There was good faith there regarding Ireland but not a good understanding of all that was involved.

Ireland felt that Leo's efforts showed only that he was siding with England. However, when later the nationalist forces in Ireland opened a boycott, the pope told the Catholics there that it was their duty to obey the laws of the country. State authority must be obeyed, and he directed the priests to tell the people so, and also to tell them to present

their demands in a more orderly manner. This had some
effect on Ireland. Also it stopped Gladstone's angry speeches,
and later, when the queen celebrated her golden jubilee,
Cardinal Ruffo-Scilla was sent to London to represent the
pope and found a cordial welcome awaiting him.

In Russia the situation between pope and czar had begun
to improve as early as 1880. There had been no concordat
operating with Russia since 1865, when an angry Pius IX
ordered from his presence the Russian chargé d'affaires. In
1882 a new concordat was signed. Exiled Polish priests and
bishops were released and returned to their dioceses, while
freedom of worship was restored to the Poles. In 1883 Alexander III was crowned and the pope sent Cardinal Van-
nutelli to represent him. Some ten years later Alexander
Iswolsky was appointed minister plenipotentiary to the Holy
See.

Prussia and England were of course Protestant countries
and Russia was Orthodox. Where France and Italy were
concerned matters were very different, for even though they
were by tradition Catholic, their governments were certainly no longer Catholic. The sad fact was that many in
both countries were not merely trying to keep the Church
in its own sphere, or what they considered its sphere, but
were hoping it would soon pass out of existence altogether.
It had had its years, even its centuries of value—that they
granted. Now it was only an old and useless institution to
followers of the Enlightenment. And, sadly true, and difficult
to argue down, was the fact that during the long years when
Pius IX was on the throne the Church seemed to be doing
little to aid the common people.

In France many still remembered the old regime when
kings taxed the people unmercifully in order to keep themselves in palaces and fine attire, when prelates as well as
nobles lived in luxury, when sometimes a cardinal was sec-

ond only to the king in the size of estates. As for Italy, where the papacy had lost nearly all its proud possessions, it was unthinkable that those who now owned them would willingly or unwillingly return anything.

There were popular heroes in Italy but they were Garibaldi and Crispi. For the moment the fact that the new industrial age was bringing a new poverty with it and making a new aristocracy was overlooked. Liberty and freedom and the brotherhood of man were the catchwords. In France Gambetta was calling the Church the eternal enemy. The Freethinkers in Naples met to speak against the "dogmas based on a revelation which was only an outworn superstition of the past." In Paris the pope was called by some a "dangerous deceiver." The general feeling was that the new world would soon put aside all these outgrown ideas.

Leo felt especially sad that France, a country he loved, should be so estranged. He knew that, despite revolutions and socialistic fever, there was another France, one which showed itself most strongly in its devotion to mission work in far lands. So long ago as 1846, on his way from London back to Rome, he had stopped in Paris and seen for himself that religion there was forging ahead in its social service work and was also making intellectual progress. He had found in the clergy a strong sense of faith and it was clear this had not died out under the brief republic or under the last Napoleon. Leo had felt antagonism toward him and this had grown with the years, but he knew the solid core of faith was still alive in the oldest daughter of the Church.

When in 1881 Gambetta and his new ministry were again confiscating the goods of the religious orders, Cardinal Guilbert of Paris had objected energetically but with no results. Leo himself wrote a stirring letter to the cardinal, not inveighing against the regime but praising the mission work of French Catholics, the many hospitals, the orphanages and asylums which had been built all over the world for the poorest of the poor—and by the alms of the French people and the unselfish love of French missionaries. Catholic France had given her funds and her people both for the love of God.

The letter did no good except to hearten the people to whom it was addressed. Cardinal Guilbert followed it with a letter of his own: "I am a very old man and I have seen in my lifetime the political forms of my country change seven times. But remember that the Church has known greater dangers than the present. She lives still in the hearts of France and will be present at the burial of those who plan to annihilate her."

However, to many it looked as if the end of the Faith was at hand in France. The new order considered marriage no sacrament. The education of children was being taken out of Church hands. Secular subjects only were taught in the state schools. No schoolbook mentioned religion. No crucifix could be hung in any classroom. Religious teachers were forced out and some expelled entirely. The Carthusians had been driven from their ancient Grande Chartreuse. More and more restrictions were being passed against monks and priests. France's anticlericalism had become almost a religion, and Dumas, hearing Gambetta speak and seeing the people hanging on his vivid words, said he was acting "like a god for those who have no God."

In 1883 the government in France banned religious orders entirely, to the sorrow of the pope, who wrote an appeal to the president of that country: "The events which have been occurring for some time past in France regarding religious matters cause Us serious apprehension and deep concern." He spoke of the loss of religious education—"to banish

from a nation of thirty-two million Catholics religious education from its schools." He protested at the same time the laws
on divorce and on the forcing of military service on the
clergy.

The president replied, admitting the justice of the pope's
appeal regarding antireligious feeling in France. But he
added that surely one remedy lay with the pope himself—
to insist on an attitude of political neutrality on the part of
the clergy as well as of the monarchist groups among the
Catholic laity. That, of course, was merely his opinion, he
added. The real answer must come from his ministers to
whom he had given the pope's letter.

Both letters were dignified. It was true that the pope had
right on his side, but it was also true that many in France
who were now in power feared that the republic would be
in danger if it gave in at all to Rome. The Bourbon prelates
were always hoping to restore the heirs of the old monarchy
and the heirs were never very far away.

In 1880 the pope had issued an encyclical letter on Christian marriage—*Arcanum divinae sapientiae*—plainly aimed at
the countries where this sacrament was no longer considered
such by the government. First he pointed out the unity and
perpetuity of marriage from historical beginnings, its progressive corruption, its restoration to dignity by Christ, and
now its recorruption by the present-day enemies of religion.
He condemned utterly such forces as were at work to break
down the marriage bonds, the unity and indissolubility of
marriage, and he urged the bishops fully and soundly to
instruct the faithful and make clear to them that marriage was a sacramental contract. There were, he said clearly,
matters on which the state had rights but there were also
matters of faith where the Church was above the state.

In the same year he had written another encyclical—
Sancta Dei civitas—which was both an appreciative state-

ment and an appeal for missionary enterprises and especially for the Society for the Propagation of the Faith, whose needs were many and constantly growing, and for whose aid France had sent so many religious and given so much money. He asked aid for those deprived of teachers as well as of bread—"the harvesters are few—let them be not fewer in the future," he pleaded.

In Italy the Roman Question was still the center of everything. The Vatican had put out a few feelers regarding some reconciliation. A considerable number of government officials wanted something done about the many petty annoyances which had resulted from it. For a few years a kind of underground negotiation went on. Small gestures were made which looked as if they might lead to larger results. When the king visited other cities the prelates made him welcome. In Florence the archbishop embraced him and gave him his blessing.

Then something happened. Some said it was the Jesuits' interference, that it was well known they were urging Leo to restore papal authority over Rome. Others said Freemasonry had objected so strongly that the government gave way and even the small gestures were given up, which was no doubt the real reason. One fact was certainly and definitely correct—Freemasonry was the chief force against the Church and many of the hostile leaders came from this organization. Pius had known it and Leo faced it. This was not merely an opponent with whom to argue. This was an enemy, an implacable enemy with whom no peace or even truce could be made.

In April of 1884 Leo published an encyclical, very different from the earlier ones which had been persuasive in tone. This one was harsher and coldly logical. In *Humanum genus* he spoke openly of Freemasonry. In no uncertain terms he called it "a huge evil," one which had as its aim the destruction of religious values and which might well pull down the basic moral laws. To its members God did not exist at all. His church on earth was not a necessity for mankind but a nuisance standing in the way of their plans as benefactors of mankind. They spoke no word of duty to the Creator. They spoke only of a duty to human beings, a thing which could be altered with the political regime of the land or the year, whereas the law of God, the moral law, was divine and therefore unalterable. Their doctrine led to religious indifference and at times they declared their intention to uproot religion entirely. But worst of all was their fundamental doctrine—the separation of reason from any supernatural revelation.

The Masonic doctrine, Leo stated, gave no positive certainty about the soul or immortality. Its teaching was naturalistic. The state was to be in control of matters which the Church considered sacramental. Leo had said these things in his earlier and much gentler statement about Freemasonry issued in 1878. This time he forbade Catholics to join and he urged the study of Christian philosophy as a protection against error. He recommended the Third Order of St. Francis to Catholics and also hoped that there would soon be some sort of restoration of Catholic guilds among workers.

He called on the people of the Church not to listen to this unhappy doctrine and urged the clergy everywhere to make it very clear exactly why it was forbidden to join the Masonic sect. And he also made it clear that when he spoke of Freemasonry he did not indict individual Masons. His work was to fight error and at the same time pity the erring, the mistaken, the ones lured to strange paths. These were ignorant of the real aim of the leaders, which was a weaving of plots to abolish both throne and altar if these did not yield

to their demands. "Pride and ambition and vanity can darken
the keenest intellect," Leo said.

The pope had been very careful about some of the stories
told by credulous Catholics about the rites of Masonry. Some
of them were so absurd that it was obvious they would die
out in due time and they did. But one story provided all sorts
of emotional implications while it lasted, and that was the
story of Diana Vaughan and her book. It was supposedly
written by a certain Taxil, who pretended to have been a
Mason but who was now a Catholic. Diana had made to him
all sorts of revelations regarding the Masons—tales of a
devil's workshop, of devil worship, of magical practices—
and all her revelations were solemnly set down by her
biographer.

The book had a remarkable success in some European
countries. France was greatly roused by it but Germany and
Italy remained for the most part sceptical. However, the
book did produce one anti-Masonic congress at Trent. Eventually, when he thought the matter had gone too far, Leo
charged the Holy Office with an investigation.

Before they were fairly started, word came from Paris.
Taxil had made a cynical address in a music hall there and
explained that there had never been a Diana at all. She was
the figment of his vivid imagination. He had just been making fun of Catholics and of everyone else who could be
fooled.

The excitement died down but it took time. In fact, on the
very day that Diana became fiction and not fact the Vatican
received a letter from an excited Italian Catholic. He had
just been reliably informed that both Diana and her biographer had been murdered by Freemasons in the offices of the
Paris Geographical Society!

Even by the early 1880's the pope's methods had become very clear in Catholic countries and in others, too. It was evident that he felt his special mission was to calm prejudice and hatred against the papacy by definite means—by elevating the standard of culture among priests; by improving the seminaries; by showing the Church encouraged science; by explaining that the Church was not the enemy of civil sovereignty; and by showing that the Church had a deep and loving interest in the working people of the world.

Chapter Ten

LIKE Pius IX, Leo had refused to accept the annual monetary indemnity that the Italian government offered to his predecessor in payment for the losses in Rome. Like Pius, Leo had remained a voluntary prisoner in the Vatican. He could have, of course, decided against continuing this but he did not. It had been a dramatic gesture in the eyes of the world and especially of the Catholic world where many were troubled about their faith and swayed by the new ideas which had in them some good but also much of evil.

Leo knew that the monetary payment was no guarantee at all for the future. "Those who give it to us today can take it away again tomorrow," he said. And, just as Pius had stated it, Leo knew that some day the Holy See must insist on full dominion over a certain area in Rome, even though a small one. This was no mere Italian affair. It affected every Catholic in the world. Therefore there would have to be a legal settlement and not merely the offer of a handful of lire.

Some years before in a pastoral issued at Perugia Cardinal Pecci had written of the claim of the papacy to temporal rule. He said there must be something tangible in its possession, since without certain temporal rights the pope would be always at the mercy of whatever government was in command at any one time, perhaps a kindly one, perhaps not. "He who looks after the highest end, the spiritual, cannot in reason be a subordinate of those who are working for material ends which are in fact only means to the highest, the spiritual," he had written.

In Rome the social world was divided. Black Rome, made up chiefly of those who held offices at the papal court, paid no attention to the upstart royal court, nor did White Rome, the royal party, pay any attention to the out-dated papal groups. To the papal group there was no king of Italy. To them he was still the Duke of Savoy.

Even so, the royal family still held to the forms of the Faith. When one of the king's daughters was to be married, no church was ready to hold the ceremony. The pope was also the bishop of Rome and the churches were under his jurisdiction. Then someone remembered one small church not under papal rule; it was the property of the state as a public monument. There the marriage took place.

Even more complicated was the situation when a king or other chief of state came from a foreign country and wanted to pay his respects to both king and pope. The Vatican could not receive him if he went first to the king, since this was a matter of precedence. When Wilhelm of Prussia was to visit the pope after seeing the king, he went first to the Prussian legation building. Then, since this was considered part of his homeland, he rode in a Prussian carriage and from a Prussian building to the Vatican. He had gone from his own home and so symbolically satisfied the code.

Serbia, which had no legation in Rome, solved the matter in another way. King Alexander went to a hotel, which made that temporary extraterritorial Serbian jurisdiction. Then he drove to the Vatican. Later the papal secretary came to return the call.

In 1880 Leo had to choose a new secretary of state, when Cardinal Nina was forced to resign because of impaired health. In his place the pope chose Cardinal Jacobini, whom he had known before his election to the papacy and who had aided him in matters connected with the Austrian and German churches.

The Vatican decided the time had come to place the remains of Pius IX in San Lorenzo where he had asked to be buried. Government and municipal authorities were notified that the removal was to be carried out. It was agreed that this be done at night, and late, because there would be fewer people about and less chance of trouble. No police protection was suggested or asked for.

Somehow the news had spread and when at midnight the cortege moved down the streets, followed by thousands of the faithful come to honor the dead pope, a mob also formed, throwing stones, cursing, screaming, all the two hours it took to go to San Lorenzo. "Throw him into the Tiber," some shouted. "Throw his gang in, too," yelled others. The mourners went along in silence, following the plain bier. It was no doubt their peaceful attitude and lack of any retorts that prevented a riot.

Leo set down his own feelings about the disgraceful matter and with an indignant pen: "If the remains of Pius IX cannot be borne through this city without shameful disorder and rioting, who will guarantee that such violence would not break out should We appear on the streets? Therefore it will be more and more a thing well understood that We can now remain alive in Rome only by remaining a prisoner shut up in the palace of the Vatican."

In other countries than Italy there was continuing distrust of the papacy. In France, the papacy ceased to be of any importance save among the tight little groups of monarchists, and even they were divided into Legitimists, Orleanists and Bonapartists. France was a republic now—and fiercely anticlerical.

As for the Roman Question it was as far from being answered as the day it was first brought forward. Most Italian authorities would no doubt have been happy to see something done on both sides for it caused continual trouble. The Church would not as yet permit Catholics there to vote or to have any share in the government, for, as Leo phrased it, "justified reasons." He did add that generally speaking, a total abstention from political life would be blameworthy since it would mean a refusal to share in co-operation for the common good. But it was obvious he felt the time had not come.

Leo saw that, in general, things could not be pushed. He understood thoroughly that time could not be turned back, that old regimes were gone and that a new world was at hand. Even so he was very definite as to where he gave his support and where he asked for support. He sympathized with the new cultural aims, just as he was ready to recognize various kinds of governments, provided they were stable and would not interfere with the basic tenets of the Church. Freemasonry did and this he opposed vigorously.

He was not, however, as immovable as Pius had been. If a country became a republic and Catholics could live in peace there and practice their religion, if the Church could function freely, that was enough. The things of Caesar's, the material matters, were one thing. The things of God were another.

When he realized there would be no immediate chance of any reconciliation with the Italian state, he took the matter up in other ways. To rulers and legates who called at the Vatican he talked about possible support for the restitution of some of the papal territories. The Catholic Church had now no central base save the Vatican area itself.

He spoke to the Austrian ambassador, but in vain, for that country belonged to the Triple Alliance, the other partners being Germany and Italy. When the kaiser, son of the first Wilhelm, came to call, he, too, turned aside the request diplomatically. His country was a part of the Triple Alliance and so had bonds with the government of Italy and must act with them.

Not too disappointed, Leo turned elsewhere. He knew new alliances might be formed in the future, new governments in fact. And he had won in small ways, as when he had taken the side of Russia in a dispute with the Poles—an action which was later to lead to the restoration of a Russian envoy to the Vatican.

Again ambassadors were being appointed to the Vatican— slowly at first but in gradually increasing number. More Leo could not do. Some of his efforts were crowned with success only by later popes, but he had laid the ground work. His adroit negotiations, his courtesy, the admission that others had rights and sometimes justification, were to have their results in the future.

In 1881 Alexander, czar of Russia, was assassinated. He had been responsible for the freeing of serfs in Russia and for other humanitarian measures. He was killed by the terrorists against whom he had waged a bitter opposition. On the day of his death he had signed a new and liberal constitution for his country.

Leo expressed his deep sorrow at this murder. "All Europe is filled with horror at this dastardly crime," he wrote, "and We are troubled because there have been other threats against other princes of Europe." He immediately sent Cardinal Jacobini to take his condolences to the two Russian princes who were visiting Rome at the time, and sent a letter to the new emperor, Alexander III, who responded with a note of appreciation.

Only a few months later came word of the assassination of President Garfield of the United States. Cardinal Jacobini wrote to Secretary Blaine of the Holy Father's profound sorrow and Blaine in answer spoke of the grief of both Catholics and Protestants at the president's death.

The next year came another death, but this a natural one, that of Garibaldi, the leading figure in the Risorgimento. When Leo was told of it, he was silent for a moment, then he said softly, "God be merciful to him." The prayer for one of his bitterest enemies was the pope's only revenge.

In an encyclical in 1885—*Immortale Dei* which was on the Christian constitution of state—Leo was to refer to these murders. He spoke of the legitimacy of all forms of government and he cited the examples of the early Christians who did not try to overthrow the ruling authority. He addressed himself to the legitimists of all lands who claimed the cause of the Church must be bound up with monarchy. Speaking simply but explicitly, he said that "there is no reason why the Church should not approve the sovereignty of either one or the other . . . that various peoples select the form of government which best suits their natures . . . that no city can live without a government . . . a necessity which Christians regard as a creation of God. He who exercises authority is a representative of God, but he must do it for the common good and not his own advantage."

He quoted Thomas Aquinas' definition of law—a reasonable disposition made in the name of the good of all and promulgated by the one who is in charge of the community. There was of course, added Leo, one occasion, one reason, and only one, that allowed men to be disobedient to their governments, and that was when something asked of the people was at variance with divine or natural laws. Again he pointed to the early Church whose members did not revolt against their governments but stood out against interference with their religious rights.

In the encyclical he spoke out, however, and very definitely, on the subjects of socialism, communism and nihilism, which he said could never be true governments—"for they mean the death of civil society." But the Church of Christ, he said, could not be "suspicious of princes nor disliked by peoples."

The exhortation against revolution pleased several governments, especially Russia, because of the Poles, and England, because of the Irish. It did not please some Catholics to whom this looked like far too much leaning to liberalism. But the pope forestalled such criticism by saying: "If every period of dissension among Catholics has proved harmful, then it would be all the more so in our time, when the Church is faced with so many impassioned enemies."

He had not waited long after he became pope to show an interest in establishing some rapport with the Eastern Christians. In 1880 the Slavic people celebrated the millennium of two of their saints, Cyril and Methodius. Both of them died in communion with the Holy See and one was buried in Rome. They were revered as saints by both East and West.

Leo wrote a brief encyclical in September of that year, extending the cult of the two saints to the entire world and endowing their feast day with a solemn office in the calendar. He wrote of the apostolic labors of the two men, of their invention of the Cyrillic alphabet, of their personal connection with the Holy See.

Many from Slavic lands wrote to thank him for his courtesy. Many others came to Rome for the celebration of the thousandth anniversary of their beloved saints. The audience granted them by the pope was very colorful—the pope in white, the cardinals in scarlet, the long lines of Slavonic pilgrims, the nobles in rich garments, the peasants in white linen jackets with scarlet sleeves, the women with gay kerchiefs on their heads. The Swiss guards added their black and yellow uniforms to the brilliant scene. When the pope spoke to the pilgrims he ended, "When you go home tell your people that you have seen Us open Our hearts to you, that the Slavic nations are objects of Our affection—and convey to them all Our apostolic benediction."

Leo established a hierarchy for Bosnia and Herzegovina. He founded in the Roman seminary chairs for the teaching of everything pertaining to the Greek liturgy, something which drew so many students that a few years later a new wing had to be added to the college. In 1881 he had set up a Bohemian college in Rome and, by agreement with the Prince of Montenegro, he restored the Greek seminary. He sent Monsignor Cretoni, secretary of the Propaganda, to Constantinople on a special mission. He raised an Armenian prelate to the cardinalate—the first from that area in four hundred years to be a member of the Sacred College. He opened communications with the Shah of Persia, since a number of Catholics lived in that country. In 1884 he restored the ancient See of Carthage and later named its archbishop a cardinal. Later still he was to establish a Catholic hierarchy in India, and in Egypt four new apostolic vicariates in the care of the Society of African Missions. One great hope he still cherished—to set up two central schools in Athens and in Constantinople.

His attempt to establish friendly relations directly with Japan and China failed, in part because for many years Christian nations had used those lands for their imperialistic purposes. Yet the result in Japan was not exactly a failure for the missionaries remained close to the people. In China the French government insisted all intercourse be carried on through its embassy. For the time being the pope ceased his efforts there.

In 1883 Leo was at last able to carry out the promise he had made a few years before and opened the Vatican archives for the use of scholars everywhere. During that time he had also dealt with the Vatican library itself, as well as with the manuscripts and papers in the archives. The library there had actually been begun at Avignon but, when the popes returned to Rome, very little of the fine collection came with them. A great many of the books had been bought by the Borghese family and these Leo purchased back from them to place in the Vatican library again. He also gave many new volumes, bought by him personally, including the breviary of Petrarch.

Over the years since the library had functioned in Rome, various popes had added to it but it was under Eugene IV that it became a really important collection of books. Sixtus V had given the library a new and costly home of its own but it had its disadvantages, one the fact that scholars who pored over the manuscripts had very little light to see by. In fact, one side of the long narrow room had only a single window. Yet for three hundred years scholars had managed to work there. Now Leo built a new reading room with lofty windows which gave excellent light. When, later on, this proved too small for the increasing number of scholars, a new reading room was built and the former room was used to house the manuscripts and papers.

When these were being filed correctly—an immense task—many fascinating documents came to light and unexpected treasures were found. When one man was restoring a palimpsest—that is, a vellum used twice—he found under the second writing the original of Cicero's long lost *de Republica*.

Among the papers was a manuscript letter to Ann Boleyn from Henry VIII, a script dated 1206 containing the first mention of Greenland, and one of 1493, concerning the voyage of "Cristofor Colom."

These archives, called secret, of course had never been exactly that. Certain scholars had been able to open them for purposes of study and historical research, but many of them had never been examined. It would have required long and hard work to go through them and catalogue them, not only the literary manuscripts but the legal papers of the early popes, the briefs between crowns and popes, many of them not only signed but with beautiful seals affixed.

It troubled some people very much to have all this opened to all scholars, no matter of what faith, and their objections were vocal. They feared that some of this material, if seen by people inimical to the Church, might turn out to show the Church in a bad light. There were expressions of real horror from those who thought all this might lead to the making public of things discreditable to both Church and papacy.

When Leo heard of some of these objections, he said with irritation, "There are people who would keep Peter's betrayal out of the Gospels." He had been not too annoyed when he was told how fearful some were about his idea. "*Testi piccoli*," he called them—small brains—and continued serenely with his plans. "One need never fear the truth," he said. To a German history club delegation which came to see him, he said, "Go as far back as you can to the sources and do not be afraid of the publication of documents."

Just before the rooms were opened Leo wrote a papal letter to several cardinals, among them Cardinal Hergenröther, just appointed archivist, in which he spoke of truth as the objective of history, and stated that to make it historically reliable much laborious investigation, maturity of judgment and critical discernment are necessary. That, he said, was why he was throwing the entire Vatican library and archives open to historical research and encouraging the participation of all scholars in such work.

He wrote that it was his great desire that the clergy unite the study of the humanities with their theological studies. He wanted not only a few but a great many well educated. He wanted to see education at all levels. He had felt this when he was at Perugia, and he still thought so.

It was very true that this action of opening the library archives had won sympathy from many who had not previously been cognizant of or greatly interested in papal matters, among them the people of the press. The correspondent of the *London Times* and the editor of *Petit Paris* had asked to see him and to both he had given interviews. But perhaps the most unusual interview was one he granted a woman journalist, Madame Severine, recommended to the pope by an artist who had painted his portrait. She wrote the pope a fine letter asking for an audience. She wrote of her admiration for His Holiness' solicitude for the disinherited of the earth. This, so in harmony with the spirit of Christ, so encouraging for those who dreamed of brotherhood, gave her the courage to ask something of His Holiness which no other Catholic had thought to ask.

When she came, she told him that what she wanted was a pronouncement on anti-Semitism and he talked with her at length on that subject. She wrote in her interview that she had found him less of a sovereign and more of an apostle, and he seemed most of all like a grandfather.

When she spoke of religious wars, he said, "But they are two contradictory words."

"Then shall we say racial wars, Your Holiness?"

"What races?" asked Leo. "They are all sons of Adam

whom God created. What if they differ in color and aspect? They are moulded from the same spiritual substance."

She had not told him her interview would not be printed until he had seen it. As a result there were some inaccuracies. Her interpretation was not always what he had intended to convey to her, especially when he used the phrase, "My kingdom is not of this world."

He said nothing unkind about the results of the interview. Her printed story showed, he said, "a liveliness of imagination. I am sure she thought I said what she wrote." But he became much more circumspect about giving interviews.

In 1883, in preparation for October, the month of the Rosary, Leo issued an encyclical letter—as he was to do in future almost yearly during that month—urging on the universal Church a dedication to the devotion, so great, so confident, to the Queen of Heaven. It was a devotion, he wrote, which was always most important when the militant church of God was endangered by the violence of heresy and moral corruption or by the attacks of powerful enemies. Her very titles proved that—Victory, Peace Giver, Consoler, Helper.

The need of such help was perhaps never more necessary than now, perhaps not since the time when the great Dominic introduced the use of the rosary, and Leo asked that October have "special and splendid services, that people visit churches to pray the rosary with the intention that Christians and civil society be delivered from dangers and restored to the longed-for peace."

In Africa the missions were flourishing and Leo was in constant touch with Cardinal Lavigerie, in whose capable hands the work was still placed. Leo's hope was to make his

see the center of a vast antislavery campaign. Even though
blackbird ships were no longer bringing captives to the
United States, Arab slave traders were still taking people
by force from their native villages, to the number, it had
been estimated, of many thousands a year, selling them in
South American countries, especially Brazil.

In the 1880's the Dark Continent was being rediscovered
by European nations. There had been some colonization but
the actual taking over of parts of the continent came later
and after those nations were no longer making fortunes in
slaves. But the slave trade still continued. In 1884 Cardinal
Lavigerie had called attention to it at a conference on African affairs held by all the large western nations in Berlin. It
was agreed then that vigorous efforts be made to end the
trade entirely.

The pope sent funds to aid the crusade and urged that
missionary bands from every land send some of their members to work in Africa. He urged that antislavery committees
be set up everywhere; one had been set up in Rome. The
response from the missioners was gratifying. Everywhere
there was an awakening and a realization of the situation. Leo himself wrote a short encyclical on the subject,
addressed in particular to the bishops of Brazil, but meant
for everyone to read. Surely, he said, there must be effectual
methods to wipe out "this inhuman commerce. It fills Us with
horror to hear that even today 40,000 Africans with no consideration for age or sex, are torn from their homes by force
and, chained and beaten, are dragged a thousand miles to
markets where they are exhibited and sold."

He reviewed the history of slavery, the work of Christianity in trying to end it, the opposition of more than one
pope to this shameful traffic. And he ended by urging slaves,
when they were freed, to a right use of their precious liberty.

Later in that same year Cardinal Lavigerie brought a pil-

grimage from Africa to thank the pope for his efforts—
twelve missionaries and twelve ransomed slaves. It was the
first time that Christian Negroes from the very center of
Africa had appeared there.

Eventually the power of the Arab traders in western lands
was broken, not ended entirely, but the world's attention
was now fixed on it and it grew weaker continually. "Africa
will some day," William Pitt had said in the House of Commons years before, "repay by her intelligence and her
virtues the debt owed other nations by their efforts for
her redemption," a statement with which Leo could agree
wholeheartedly.

The year 1887 marked Leo's golden jubilee as a priest and
it was made a truly magnificent celebration.

Fifty years before Don Vincenzo Pecci had said his first
Mass in a little chapel in Rome. Now, as Peter's successor, he
was to celebrate a Pontifical High Mass at the altar of St.
Peter's. Even in hostile Rome everything was set to make
it a great day. The city authorities were on their best be-
havior. Duke Torlonia, the mayor of the city, in the name of
the city councilors, offered the pope the congratulations and
good wishes of the city of Rome on his jubilee. It was understood that this had the approval of the king. But when
Crispi, still premier, learned about it, he sent immediately
for the mayor, fired him forthwith from his office, and insisted the king sign the paper of dismissal. Wires carried the
news all over the world and it created a very bad impression
of the government, but one of increased friendliness for the
old pontiff.

There was much excited questioning in Rome. Would the
celebration now take place? Would public order and safety
be guaranteed if it did? The government refused to take any

responsibility for what might happen, but eventually a promise came that the streets around St. Peter's would have order
preserved, and it was decided to go ahead.

On the day of celebration the great basilica was crowded
with at least fifty thousand people, from cardinals to simple
pilgrims. At nine o'clock the jubilee Mass began. The palace
guard, the Swiss guard, were all alert as the pope, preceded
only by his cardinals, entered the basilica on his sedia. The
excitement of the great crowd was increased by the knowledge that this was the first such ceremony at St. Peter's since
1870. When the pope's chair appeared, loud cheers broke
out. Handkerchiefs fluttered, and many people wept. No one
could have stopped their exuberance. But as Leo lifted his
hand the noise died away and a hush fell over the great
building.

The pope wore the mitre presented for the jubilee by the
German emperor. When he left the basilica he was wearing
that given him by the people of Paris. He wore the chain
and cross presented by the people of Colombia and a ring
which was the gift of the Sultan of Turkey.

At first he had seemed startled by the great shouting
crowd and was seen to shrink visibly. He turned very pale
and his hand was trembling as he blessed the people. But
when he began the Mass he was as composed as if he were
celebrating in his private chapel.

After it was over and he was again on his throne, wearing
no mitre now but a magnificent tiara, the gift of the Catholics
of France, the bearers stopped before St. Peter's statue.
The cardinals gathered in a semicircle about him as he gave
the words of blessing to the people, turning from side to side
so that he had faced them all. Then the procession left St.
Peter's. Again there was a shout from those inside the church
and the many who had been waiting outside.

Leo had borne up well during the long effort. After the

blessing he was taken to the Pietà Chapel where a chair and
a prie-dieu had been placed for him. He looked very weary
now but very happy, too. Suddenly, however, he threw himself on his knees and burst into a storm of weeping. In a very
little while he managed to control his emotion and went back
to his own apartments.

From all over the world had come gifts, many of them
gifts of money to carry on his mission works. They poured
on him from everywhere, along with the good wishes of
nations, of princes, of societies, gifts from rich and poor, from
high and low.

President Cleveland wanted to send a gift with his felici-
tations and spoke to Archbishop Gibbons about it—would a
copy of the Constitution perhaps be welcome? The cardinal
assured him it would be excellent: "No one would question
its fitness, for the dissemination of the principles of our government would be above criticism," he said.

Beautifully bound in white and crimson and printed on
vellum, it was presented by Archbishop Ryan of Philadelphia. Leo, accepting it with evident pleasure, said, "Toward
America I have a special love. Your government is free, your
future full of hope."

The German emperor sent a miter, the empress, a set of
vestments, Queen Victoria, a great silver bowl. A Hungarian
Jew presented a very unusual chronological calendar, and
several fine Hebrew Bibles were the gifts of rabbis. Bombay
sent a fine piece of silk and a soutane was made from it for
the pope to wear during one of the jubilee Masses.

Cuba gave a great box of the products of the land and the
Sultan of Turkey a beautiful antique pastoral ring. King
Humbert's sister gave him a magnificent cope. For the jubilee
itself Leo had worn a soutane of Irish linen, woven for this

purpose in Ireland. The lace on his rochet was the work of
Florentine nuns.

The Indians of Canada had written a congratulatory
address in an Indian tongue. From England a canon of Canterbury sent a book bound in white vellum and with the
papal arms on the cover. On the inside page Canon Jenkins
had penned a verse:

> Even as to Peter on the wave
> Who dared, yet feared, the tempest's strife,
> May Jesus' hand, stretched forth to save,
> Be the calm haven of thy life.
> Till in the kingdom of the blest,
> Whose sun shall nevermore go down,
> Thy cares shall find an endless rest,
> Thy life the faithful servant's crown.

The offerings of money from England and America and
Ireland and South America gave Leo a great opportunity to
carry out what he had been longing to do—found new missions and give sums to the poor of various lands.

From everywhere in the world had come messages and
gifts, but none came from the Quirinal to the Vatican. The
only direct notice taken of the jubilee was a letter of instruc-
tions from Crispi, saying that the Italian government would
tolerate no disturbance from pilgrims or clerical parties.

Several gifts were not of money or fine raiment or jewelry.
One was the statement of the liberation of thousands of
African slaves in Brazil, carried out in time for the jubilee.
The Africans sent a personal gift, too—two graceful gazelles,
each with a silver collar around its neck on which were engraved lines written by Cardinal Lavigerie. And one gift
came from his own Carpineto. His townspeople sent him a
flock of snow-white goats and a shepherd to care for them.

Carpineto had been much in his thoughts during that year

of jubilee. While he was still at Perugia he had learned that the town's supply of water was very low and he had a fresh supply brought from nearby springs. Only a year ago he learned that the supply was again dangerously low and he had commissioned a firm to locate newer and better sources. They had been found and on the day he celebrated his jubilee Mass he was told the work was completed.

Carpineto now rejoiced in a fine supply of water. An inscription on the public fountain said, "His Holiness, Pope Leo XIII, caused this most salubrious water to be brought here," and under that was a felicitous little verse by the donor himself.

Chapter Eleven

THOUGH Leo had never made any attempt to undo the ruling against participation by Catholics in the government of Italy, he encouraged their participation in social works. More than one club had his approval and his interested attention.

It was still a time when many considered the Church a spiritual power that had little interest in the material welfare of the working classes. The socialists, who had made the problem of the workers their own, said that truth was in man and not in a God above time and space. Prayers would not settle such problems. They considered the Church an enemy of the workers and told them so. Christian justice was no part of Christian doctrine today, they said.

It was also true that many of the clergy, seeing this social unrest and hearing the unpleasant doctrine which socialists preached, had turned entirely from reform and so strengthened the hands of the Marxists. There were, however, many who reacted differently, among them the great archbishop von Ketteler of Mainz and Cardinal Manning who went to the aid of striking English dock workers. But they represented the minority rather than the majority. Those who had a place to live and enough to eat gave little thought to the troubles of the working class, so little, in fact, that by the

time Leo came to the papal throne, theories of socialism had
become what he called them—a deadly plague.

Counteracting the socialist appeal were the clubs formed
among Catholics in which the discussion of social justice was
the basic theme. In Rome there was the Artists and Workers
Society for Mutual Charity, the special interest of a priest
and a layman, Monsignor Jacobini and Count Vespignari.
There was also the Roman Club of Social Studies which
numbered among its members at least three who later became cardinals. Other members were a Dominican priest, a
Swiss citizen, an Austrian count. This club with its varied
national membership was the pioneer of the entire Catholic
social movement and was the forerunner of a much larger
institute. Leo was very interested in their work and received
reports of their meetings. He encouraged their research on
wages, conditions for workers, rights of private property, interest on loans, revival of the guilds and every matter which
involved social justice.

Similar clubs were operating in other countries. In France
Count Albert de Mun had founded workers clubs which
studied the reconstruction of a state built on Christian principles. One of the few aristocrats who opposed the monarchists, he had always emphasized that labor was a human
act and workingmen were not merely instruments of produc-
tion. Another of interest was "le bon Harmel," an industrialist who owned a model factory. And there was the memory
of Ozanam who had fought the Voltairean concept of the
common people as needing only "a yoke, a prod and some
hay" and whose work was perpetuated in the St. Vincent de
Paul Conferences.

In England a prime mover in social improvement was
Cardinal Manning, who had said, "Labor is a social function and not merely a commodity." He believed that if a state
protected private property it should also protect the rights

of the worker since nothing was more a man's than his labor. He had put his beliefs into action. He had gone to the docks to talk to thousands of workers engaged in a strike which was proving serious to the whole country as well as to themselves. Would they stop it if he obtained more equable conditions from the port authority, he asked, and they agreed. His mediation proved successful.

The clubs had been ahead of their time perhaps, but not very far ahead. The labor question was of constantly increasing interest. Groups formed to discuss it, including both those actively interested and those who simply wanted the Church to be abreast of the times. The chief concern was to bring back into the Church the idea of a respect due to "the most precious of all goods—human life in the person of the poor."

Marx's *Das Kapital* was now to be had in translations, but Archbishop von Ketteler of Mainz had even earlier published his own work on Christianity and the Labor Question. Its theme was: "The new mission of Christianity is to free the world from the slavery of pauperism." Between the two books was the difference which was in the future to divide the world into two camps on this question. Marx blamed everything on the capitalist system, whereas the archbishop said there must be a moral change. In Belgium and Austria and Spain the study of social justice had become a burning issue.

The pope followed it all with deep interest, happy that both in Europe and in America the idea was gathering strength, that the basis of the social problem was essentially moral and that in adjusting relations between capital and labor it was charity which must lead.

One day Bishop Mermillod of Geneva said to the pope, "I believe it will be you who will reconcile the possessing classes with the working classes, Your Holiness. And when you do this you will also be fulfilling the scriptural prophecy: In a time of wealth he made a reconciliation."

The signs of this were already visible. All these various works and ideas and efforts had existed outside the official Church but it was Leo who was soon to tie them together and make clear how one motive underlay them all.

The situation regarding the labor problem was somewhat different in the United States from that in European countries. There socialists were by no means the leaders nor did the Masonic power have the political strength it had in Europe, nor was anticlericalism an important factor.

Leo was of course very conversant with the Catholic history of the United States. He knew of Charles Carroll and how he had pledged his great fortune to the cause of liberty, and of his Jesuit cousin John Carroll, who, at the request of General Washington, had been appointed by Pius VI first bishop of Baltimore, at a time when there were only 30,000 Catholics in the United States. Now in the United States there was a cardinal and many archbishops.

Leo, extremely interested in this young country and its working people, had early in 1884 convened by apostolic letter a plenary council to meet in Baltimore. The year before he had called the American archbishops to Rome to discuss the council and plan its work. Archbishop Gibbons at the time spoke to him about a Catholic university which was being planned in Washington, and Leo was very interested. Before the archbishops returned he appointed Archbishop Gibbons to head the council, since Cardinal McCloskey was ill. Also, before they returned home, the pope gave them a full-length portrait of himself and asked to have it placed in the hall where the council was to meet so that he might, in a way, be presiding there, be with them at least in spirit.

When the hierarchy met in November, they were greeted by a cable from the pope, sending his blessing. The prelates assembled sent an immediate reply and also a greeting to the still-ailing Cardinal McCloskey.

They met for an entire month. Education of both the laity and the clergy was the chief topic for discussion. Another was the new national university of which the pope had already given his approbation. It was to be an institution where the best-known masters of the arts and sciences could come to teach, as well as the best-known theologians. It was planned to invite men of high reputation in their special fields. Some funds were already at hand to open the work, notably one gift of $300,000. A large property just outside Washington was being considered. All this information Leo received with delight.

A few years later the bishops met again to discuss the ever-growing problem of labor and especially of the groups now banding together to procure better working conditions, as well as better wages. One of the most important groups at the time was the Knights of Labor which Philadelphia tailors had founded in 1869. At first it had been more or less a secret society but this element had been dropped by 1880. In that year the Knights accepted Negroes as members. Employers, too, were welcome. In fact, it excluded from its membership only "bankers, lawyers, gamblers and stockholders."

In that same year the Knights won an important victory over the Union Pacific Railway. By 1884 it had a membership of more than seven hundred thousand. Its motto was: "The injury of one is the concern of all."

This union had been one subject discussed at the Baltimore council, but not until two years later did it become a matter for debate between opposing prelates, including an archbishop of Canada. Archbishop Taschereau had asked the pope to condemn it because it was very like a secret society. He feared it had dangerous tendencies and greatly resembled the socialist groups. The Vatican issued a mild sort of condemnation, rather a reproof than a complete objection to its methods and works. Word had come to be careful, that this group was not what its detractors were trying to prove it was, and also that its president, Terence Powderley, was a practicing Catholic.

The Knights had now so large a membership that it was felt the time had come to prove to one and all that it was no secret society as its enemies charged. It was very true, they admitted, that it had been partly so in its earlier days, but now all were welcome as members and all meetings were open.

When in 1886 the Catholic bishops met in Washington Powderley came to present a complete exposition of his Knights of Labor. When he had finished and the arguments pro and con among the prelates were over, twelve archbishops and sixty-three bishops voted in favor of the Knights and only two archbishops and three bishops against them. It was then decided to take the matter up in Rome and try to have the condemnation lifted. Archbishop Gibbons had already written a letter to the Holy Father with a full explanation regarding the matter of the Knights.

At the time Archbishop Ireland and Monsignor Keane were both in Rome. Both were much interested in the Knights and were very much on their side. They discussed them with Cardinal Simeoni who was very much opposed to the organization, as much in fact as the other two were in favor of it. He, as head of Propaganda, was powerful. He merely said coldly that the condemnation had not come from his office but from the Holy See. However, he admitted he had plenty of opinions on the Knights and that none of them was favorable.

The Americans then went to talk with Cardinal Mazzala, who had lived for years in the United States and had in fact taken out American citizenship. They found he did not favor the Knights either but he promised to get further information about them before he spoke out against them. Meantime the two Americans appealed to Archbishop Gibbons to send them documents which would put the Knights in a favorable light and show they were not socialistic or a branch of the Freemasons. This he did promptly, sending from Baltimore clippings from newspapers and letters from Catholics about them. He also wrote that an actual condemnation of the Knights would in his opinion be "a real calamity."

The Vatican was still uneasy. After all Freemasonry had proved a bitter evil and many advisers said the Knights were linked with it. This the Knights had denied, as did the American prelates who added pointedly, "and we are entrusted with the care of souls and so we know."

The two prelates in Rome decided to waste no more time on cardinals but to go straight to Leo himself. He listened carefully and then asked them to prepare a paper on the matter which he and the Roman cardinals could study. While they were doing this both Gibbons and Taschereau, who had been created cardinals in the recent consistory, arrived in Rome to receive their red hats.

Cardinal-elect Gibbons and his confreres prepared a careful paper on the subject, which was printed in both Italian and French. By that time all the American prelates save two had been won to the cause of the Knights, the two who remained adamant being the very conservative Archbishop Corrigan of New York and the equally conservative Bishop McQuaid of Rochester. A letter had arrived from Cardinal Manning, to whom Gibbons had also appealed, approving thoroughly the American defense of Powderley and the Knights of Labor. The English prelate also said that he had learned a dangerous rumor was spreading in the United States that the Catholic Church was abandoning workers' unions entirely.

The defense which Cardinal Gibbons had written was masterful. He said he had not found one thing which would ally the Knights with the Freemasons. As for strikes—"they are not the invention of the Knights." He spoke of "individual and corporate monopolies which had received recognition from the law" denied the workers. He spoke of "heartless avarice which pitilessly grinds not only men but women and children," and said that there was not one element in the Knights that united them with societies condemned by the Holy See. There was no hostility to religion or to the laws of the country either. "Must the workingmen find themselves hindered in their only means of self-defense?" he asked, and quoted Cardinal Manning: " 'The accumulation of wealth in the land, the piling up of wealth like mountains in the possession of classes or individuals cannot go on. No commonwealth can rest on such foundations.' "

Cardinal Gibbons spoke, too, of the conditions of the working people: "They want to save their souls but they must also earn a living and labor is now so organized that if they do not belong to an organization that is almost impossible," and he added a bit tartly that "the dignity of the Church demands one should not offer America ecclesiastical protection she has not asked and of which she believes she has no need."

The pope read carefully the various papers and clippings. Much of the trend of ideas exhibited there he liked, no doubt because the ideas resembled his own on labor matters. He asked Cardinal Gibbons to call on the members of Propaganda and of the Holy Office and answer their questions.

Leo himself explained to them his better understanding of matters because of the papers given him by the American prelates. "They are a young people," he told the congregations, "and the faults of healthy young people are easily corrected by time. If the Americans are able to avoid the errors of degenerate Europe I am sure they will achieve great things in the future."

It was true that one great difficulty with many members of the Vatican congregations was that America was considered with alarm, even with real fear, by many in Rome. Some now talked of the pope's sudden "Americanization." The head of Propaganda remained unreconciled. But in the end the victory went to Gibbons and Manning. Word went out that the Knights of Labor were, at least for the present, to be approved. If it was found that anything in their constitutions had the tinge of socialism or communism they would be asked to take this out. This decision was made for Canada, too, and Cardinal Taschereau accepted it.

Cardinal Gibbons had won exactly what he wanted, a benevolent neutrality. The English *Punch* printed a cartoon of Leo with Gibbons and Manning sitting facing him, and Leo was saying, "I must watch these two artful dodgers."

Manning wrote happily to Gibbons, "This is surely the new world overshadowing the old—were we prophets?" and Archbishop Ireland wrote joyously, "The people are the power and the Church must be with the people—and is."

As for Cardinal Gibbons, he wrote with the greatest joy of all, "Now labor affairs will have a safety valve and not explode some day."

During 1887 Cardinal Jacobini died and the pope appointed in his place as secretary of state Cardinal Rampolla, until then papal nuncio in Spain. He was a Sicilian, a learned

man, one of great piety, cold by nature. He proved a good
choice for Leo. He was a man of firm views but who more
than once yielded them to carry out Leo's, a man who managed situations well—so well, in fact, that one annoyed
bishop said, after an audience, "The visitor is led to say
all he knows and gets nothing in return—but goes away
delighted."

In 1888, during the year of celebration of Leo's jubilee,
there came to Rome the first great workers' pilgrimage from
France, fourteen hundred in number, with three hundred
priests and a hundred heads of industrial firms. The visitors
were a very different type from those who had previously
entered the sacred precincts. The pope received them with
obvious pleasure. It was as if he were showing the world he
was not afraid of the future, not afraid of a rising working
class. This pilgrimage showed clearly that all workers were
not revolutionaries, for here were people intent only on a
share of the dignity and the happiness of life. Leo was making the cause of the working classes a matter of conscience,
trying to make the rest of the Church realize that the social
problem was not one of charity or of donations, but one of
right and of Christian justice.

"The powerful and great have no trouble in finding protection," he had said. "The humble need someone to plead
for them or they will not be heard. Therefore the aim of any
government which is Christian should be the desire to see
its subjects paid enough to live decently."

In that same year of jubilee there was held in Rome a
great meeting of all the leaders of the Fribourg Union, a
gathering of men who were seeking a solution of the labor

problem which would be Christian and not revolutionary. It had an interesting response from Germany where the kaiser sent a letter to Leo, congratulating him on the noble way in which he was using his influence on human society, and adding that he hoped the Fribourg Union would hold its next congress in Berlin. Leo wrote in answer, thanking him for his generous suggestion, and also managing to point out very politely certain things he hoped to see carried out in Germany if the Union did meet there.

It was in the same year that he wrote an encyclical on human liberty. "True liberty," he wrote, "consists not in every man's doing as he pleases, for that would end in turmoil and confusion, but rather that all may, through the injunctions of the civil laws, more easily conform to the prescriptions of the moral law."

The supreme end to which human liberty must aspire is with God, he wrote. The Church does not reject any forms of government which serve the welfare of its people; it demands only that they be constituted not to hurt anyone and especially that they violate none of the laws of the Church.

Late that year came word of the death of the German emperor and his son telegraphed the news to the Vatican. Some time later the young emperor came to Rome and visited Leo, Cardinal Rampolla having first called at the palace of the Prussian minister where Wilhelm II was staying. The Vatican visit was a very elaborate one, including a tour of galleries, the library and other Vatican treasures. The young emperor was evidently greatly impressed, most of all by the aged pope. "There is more in that sovereign of eighteen centuries than merely a man," he said thoughtfully, as he was leaving.

Leo did not mind the individual audiences or those of a few people, but the very large ones he did not relish, chiefly because he felt he ought to give each one who came something more than a general blessing. Like a good host, he wanted to speak to each visitor and that was manifestly impossible. However, he tried and sometimes he grew very weary. Then he would decide to keep the next large audience very impersonal. He always weakened; when the first person came up to ask to kiss his ring, he granted the request. Then of course a few words had to be spoken in courtesy, for this was a guest. And then another came up and another, and so each time he found himself back in the old round.

However, when they were as vast as the one that year from France he had perforce to remain impersonal. This, the largest of his reign, was followed two years later by another and much greater one from the same country, so great that one paper called it "France at Rome." There were four thousand in the huge throng and they were led by the archbishop of Rheims. Among the pilgrims was Leon Harmel, the wealthy industrialist, and great friend of labor.

"It is as if something new had entered St. Peter's," said one amazed visitor, "a brand new social power." Another who saw the vast crowd received at the Vatican and watched this very different kind of pilgrimage streaming in, said it was truly a wonderful sight to see these workmen arriving, walking with dignity and composure—"as once did Charlemagne and Otto and Barbarossa, seeking too a new consecration and investiture."

To this great mass of people Leo spoke, and in the French which the years had made polished and fine. He gave a long, prepared talk, which was the way he preferred it, for he was no extempore speaker like his predecessor. He spoke to the pilgrims about the wonderful return to Christian principles between capital and labor and called it the best safeguard of their mutual interests and one on which private prosperity and public tranquillity depended.

"Around you, dear sons," he said, "are thousands of other workers, led astray by false doctrines, thinking to find a remedy for the evils in civil society by the destructive way. They will stain the roads on which they pass with blood and only increase their own wretchedness. They clamor for the abolition of private property as the remedy, but the remedy lies in the faithful fulfillment of the duties falling on the various classes of society." He quoted the Greek archon's warning of long ago: "'To lose the hearts of the people would be a misfortune for which the friendship of the few rich and powerful would be no compensation.'"

The French pilgrims had brought him gifts of gold and silver. He was happy to know they were designated as help for the missions. He thanked them with deep gratitude. Then he smiled at them with the lovely smile that could so irradiate the thin ascetic face. "But you have brought me one greater gift—your love," he told them.

Early in 1890 the pope suffered a deep loss in the death of his brother, Cardinal Giuseppe Pecci. This death marked the end of his immediate family—parents, sisters, brothers, all were gone and he was the only one, save for nephews and their families, still left. The Latin elegy which the pope wrote on his brother's passing was a cry from the heart:

To Giuseppe, dead.

You are secure and happy in Heaven's light.
Your brother is broken with cares and bowed with years,
Wearied with storms and many troubled days—
Remember him, be mindful of him now.

Chapter Twelve

DURING his years in Perugia Archbishop Pecci had been a close observer of the labor problem. As Leo XIII, his interest had continued and his ideas on the subject had been developing. He knew there were conditions which cried to Heaven for correction. He knew many had been led astray by the insistent shouts of the revolutionaries who promised much but who had given little to the workers save added unrest, and whose solution was violence and hatred. There was need to explain, and to a great extent to Catholics, the real position of the Church on the labor question, a thing not well understood, partly because of the actions of some of its own people.

Leo planned an encyclical on the subject. He called in cardinals, prelates and secretaries to help him, among them a small, intent scholar, Monsignor della Chiesa, who was in future years to be Pope Benedict XV.

The one thing the pope impressed on them all was that the subject must be clarified in the public mind, the Catholic mind in particular, and not be merely a matter of abstruse statements for scholars. People must know exactly what the Church stood for in regard to labor. To many it was a power which had little interest in the material welfare of the workers. Some thought social justice not a Christian doctrine at all. Some thought the Church was an actual enemy of the worker. It was very true that certain of the clergy, seeing the social unrest and hearing the unpleasant doctrine of socialism, had turned entirely from reform and were strengthening the hands of socialism by their manner. For them, too, there was need of re-education.

On the other hand, there were many who understood the situation—Archbishop von Ketteler in Germany, Manning in England, Gibbons in the United States, to name a few of the most prominent. But Leo knew well that his planned encyclical would be unpopular with wealthy and high-placed Catholics.

During the long months of preparation he worked his assistants as hard as he worked himself. It was they, of course, who provided the material by their research, who wrote out many temporary copies of the paper until at last he was satisfied with the finished product. He expected a great deal of his assistants and sometimes took unusual ways to get things done. One of them, Monsignor Bocalli, who wrote a goodly part of the encyclical, Leo one morning locked in his own private study. "Here no one will disturb you," he told him. At noon he brought him a glass of wine and some biscuits, admired the work he had done, and then locked him in again.

To Cardinal Zigliara had been entrusted the chief task, that of preparing the material. He was a Dominican and a close friend of the pope who had some years before chosen him to superintend the work on the new edition of Thomas Aquinas. His was a truly gigantic task, for the researchers had had to consider the Catholic social movement from 1878 to 1890, a time of great ferment, when many new groups and associations had developed. Hundreds of opinions from many countries had been solicited before the encyclical was considered complete in May of 1891.

The text of *Rerum Novarum* had as its basis the fact that

the social question could never be settled without religion.
The things of earth could not be understood unless one also
considered the life to come. Without that as premise, the
whole universe was nothing more than a dark and unsolvable
mystery. One had to consider that in the divine plan each
life, each human being, carried in him the stamp of God,
and thus the whole argument was really a moral issue.
Problems of power must become problems of right, since it
was the moral law by which all men live, or should live. It
was, of course, to a great extent a problem of economics, too,
as the pope well knew. But Leo was carrying it into the
moral and social field so that in his hands the question became almost a crusade against the system of labor slavery.
He reworked or had his assistants work and rework their
often too scholarly statements when he thought they were
not speaking so that all the world could understand. The
paper was written and rewritten many times before the pope
thought it was ready to be published. He knew his intention
must be made very clear. That intention was to refute the
unlawful claims of socialism, to distinguish between lawful
and unlawful claims of the workers, to determine the main
actions to be carried out, the chief points to be stressed.

Leo also wanted to dispose of, by logic, plans impracti-
cable though well meant. He wanted Catholics to get a real
understanding of the labor field. Hitherto the Church had
issued mostly the statements of scholars. These were apt to
be extremely conservative and far from practicable enough
to meet the needs of a new world even if they could be
understood by the average man. Old doctrines must be applied in clear terms to modern conditions.

He wanted to make it very clear that "every man has a
right to possess property as his own." But he made it equally
clear that the earth, even though apportioned to private
owners, did not thereby cease to minister to the needs of all

"since no one exists who does not sustain life from what the land produces."

The most fundamental principle, then, if the condition of the masses was to be improved, must be the inviolability of personal property. How, the encyclical asked, could strife between owners and masses be prevented? It must be done by the work of Christian institutions, and the encyclical quoted from the Gospels concerning the love the early Christians had for one another, rich and poor: "There was not anyone needy among them."

However, the encyclical did not dwell long on generalizations. It soon became very practical in tone. For instance, the employer of labor must never work his people beyond their strength. He must give them time for leisure and rest. Wages must be enough "to support a frugal and well-behaved wage earner." "We must," wrote Leo, "tear unfortunate laborers from the hands of these speculators who make no distinction between a man and a machine and who misuse him without limit to satisfy their grasping desire for wealth."

On his side the worker must carry out fair agreements, such as promising not to injure his employer's property or engage in violence in defense of his rights. However, it was perfectly legal for workers to join associations and to form workers' unions. Some of the ancient guilds could well be revived and their methods used, for they had been operated in the ancient Christian spirit. Such a guild renewal would aid the workers, so many of whom were today "suffering a yoke little better than that of slavery itself."

"Let it be taken for granted," he wrote, "that workmen and employers should make full agreements. But even granting that, there is still a dictate of natural justice more imperious and ancient than any bargain between men and men, and that is that wages should be enough to maintain the worker in reasonable comfort. If a workman must accept harder conditions because the employer will afford him no better, then he is a victim of force and injustice. Alone and without chance of help, he must surrender to harsh employers and their greed, so that their condition becomes repugnant to their dignity as human beings. People so downtrodden become easy prey for revolutionaries."

Most of all there was need of a great outpouring on both sides of a true Christian charity, that charity which is love and the fulfillment of the entire law of the Gospels.

The encyclical said that in life there were bound to be various ranks and stations, for in an imperfect world varying fortunes and inequalities were bound to happen: "Society cannot exist without them," Leo said, and added that to reduce all men and women to the one dead level was against nature itself. Even in the beginning of history all men were not apostles or prophets or learned men, but all were necessary to each other and all had to work together for the common welfare. It was the same today.

This, however, did not mean that men were to be treated as chattels and that the poor were to be exploited and given far less than a decent wage while their employers waxed more wealthy. No law that deserved to be called a law ever stood for that, neither divine nor human, for moral freedom was every man's greatest asset.

Labor could not be sold. It could never be given a price for it was the creative effort of each man. Labor, then, it followed logically, was an aim and end of humanity while wealth was a means only. Wealth was only loaned to man; he must use it rightly and justly. If he had great possessions, of course, he might use them for himself but he was also bound to use them for the benefit of others. His wealth made him a steward in the service of God. The rich must help the poor because they had more to give and that made a rich man's the greater duty, the higher social responsibility.

What Leo wanted to have expressed very clearly as false was Marx's idea that one class was the enemy of the other. He brought forward St. Thomas' concept that there are many stations of life, many ranks in the social order, but all must work together for the common good.

This concept would, said Leo, be extended to the state for it, too, must work for the common good and for the welfare of the workers—"It would be irrational to neglect one part of its citizens and favor the other." The state must strive to keep the peace but, when there are real evils, such as workers not having their rights made secure for them, then the state must see to it that these rights are obtained. "The state exists to support and protect natural rights and not to destroy them," said the encyclical.

The final summing up of his arguments was: "The condition of the working classes is the pressing question of today and on working this out depends the welfare of society."

The encyclical was promptly acclaimed for the wonderful work it was. It received far more applause than Leo had expected. Both Catholics and Protestants called it the Magna Carta of labor and its author was dubbed Father of Workers.

Many, of course, felt far less than kind about it—for example, the parishioner of a London church where part of it was being read from the pulpit at Mass, who strode out angrily muttering, "Socialism, nothing but socialism." Some said they did not like being denounced by an old man in another land who, said one irritated industrialist, "had probably never signed a check." Some thought to end his nonsense by stopping the gifts of money to the Church. But the Anglican Bishop of Manchester said, "The pope has put his finger on the sore spot of our social system. His words must be listened to or the world will expiate its crimes by some terrible calamity."

In France the encyclical caused a veritable sensation. M.

Barres, a leading socialist, said, "A few years given to effacing existing evils as he suggests and democracy would no longer see an enemy in the priest." One newspaper said, "Up to this time the Church has been in the camp of the rich—now it passes into that of the poor." A German socialist said Leo had "resolved the social question as far as any existing person can," and added that he was ahead of princes and presidents in doing so.

Conservatives in various lands spoke out against it. They said he was rousing demagogues among the masses. "Let sleeping dogs lie," was their advice. Some thought it would lead people to demand far too much. When Leo heard that, he said, as he had said before, "These people are too old for me." When he received a group of Roman nobles in audience, he praised their continuing faithfulness to the Holy See—"and now you must each of you carry a stone to help build the new social structure of society." If they did not like his suggestion, at least no one said so.

Some among the socialists thought little of his ideas. They had their own theories and one was that metaphysical arguments were not needed to bring about the good life. On the other hand, seasoned revolutionaries, disliking his appeal to law and order everywhere, called him a real enemy of the people—this no doubt because Leo had not been content to speak only of the economic field. The real appeal, the one socialists and Marxists alike resented, was for social and moral actions he claimed necessary to bring about a change. He made it a crusade against labor slavery, against the sad results of the machine age, where the machine, which had been expected to free the worker, had instead made him a new kind of slave.

The really surprised people were the Catholic workers. Here at last was a pope who understood them and their problems, who criticized what was wrong with capitalism and urged the workers to organize into associations in order to improve their condition. Those who had worked hard and long to build up a movement for the Catholic workers, who had been often rebuffed, were the ones who read the encyclical with deepest interest and with real joy. "He stretches out his hand like a father to bless us," said one Catholic worker.

Someone pointed out that Leo had for years been carrying out in small ways what he had now written about in a large way—in new schools, free kitchens for those out of work, night asylums with free beds for those who had no homes or work. Perhaps one of the best statements of all was found in an anonymous letter to an English magazine: "One of the makers of history has entered the scene."

Leo had set down only general laws and general hopes. Before long queries came from everywhere asking for more specific statements. Should there not be a family wage? If a man had two houses should he not get rid of one if he did not need it? This rather odd question was put often and by both clergy and laity and evidently in good faith. Should workers with no children get as much wages as those who had none or were unmarried? What were the limits of workers' rights? When should the state interfere? What about some forms of insurance in case of sickness?

Leo was well aware that he could not answer queries like these. They would have to be the results of actions by governments. His was a general plea for justice. Even when the archbishop of Malines asked him to speak on a family wage, he answered that justice must be the base and not abuse. It was not an answer that pleased everyone, but Leo was not trying to make legal rulings. He was trying to awaken the conscience of the world. He explained that he had laid down only a broad design. "If I were to pronounce on any single matter of a prevailing economic problem," he wrote, "I should be interfering with the freedom of men to work out their own affairs. Certain cases must be solved in the domain of facts, case by case as they occur ... men must realize in deeds those things, the principles of which have been placed beyond dispute ... these things one must leave to the solution of time and experience." Intervention by him in giving an answer to any special case would in a way be imposing his own opinion—"That would mean I was restricting the freedom of people."

One very important thing the encyclical had done was to make workers realize that they had rights, and employers that they had duties. It gave a great impetus to the movement for social justice at that time spreading among many Catholic groups. He had stated the basic morality of the labor question. The answers must be worked out slowly and no doubt painfully.

The basic fact that had emerged from the letter was that the voice from the Vatican which many had thought was stilled forever and which many thought spoke only for those in high places and of great wealth, was speaking, in clear assured tones, for the people who were in low places and had no wealth, no influence. Leo had cleared the road for Catholic participation in modern social movements. He was called by some the Pope of the Left, but the fact was that he had the mind of a good conservative who blessed the formation of labor unions and encouraged friendly relations between capital and labor.

Books on the subject began to appear. Discussion groups increased. In France there were, within a few years after the encyclical appeared, six hundred trade unions and there were

many in Belgium. In Germany the Kolping Society flour-
ished, as it was to do for many years until Hitler suppressed
it. In Italy the trade unionists rose to a million members, and
continued until they were suppressed by Mussolini. Groups
met in Rome. Among them were not only workers but priests
and nobles. The Vatican court had become a pleasant place
for devotees of economics and social science.

By that time the movement had a name—Christian Democracy—used for the first time at a Belgian Catholic Congress in 1893, and by Verhaeren, the people's poet. Leo had
said that he would himself not have used any special name,
for he felt that, if democracy were to be really Christian, that
alone would give it a future of peace and of glory. But apparently the name meant a great deal, especially to the
younger workers, and he realized that the title signified
a democratic movement working in a definitely Christian
cause.

At first the ruling classes and those with large investments
had been the objectors to the encyclical, but as time went on
criticism of the trade unions began to grow among the workers themselves. Some who had made common cause in the
interests of the justice for which the pope spoke, grew
nervous and withdrew. There were growing fears that this
whole movement was really a flouting of the best traditions
of Catholic action. Several people appealed to the pope
personally, asking him to change some of his own dicta because they were in danger of being misapplied, and expressing their fear that he had been terribly mistaken in speaking
so openly for labor. The statements might in the future lead
to real disaster. Some were, in fact, envisaging the proletariat
as a vast army which would in the end precipitate a social revolution—"a class war against the upper classes," one
wealthy landowner told him.

Leo felt that all were entitled to voice their objections.

He knew that some of the cardinals were very uneasy about the growing debates. After some years of listening to questions and complaints, he appointed a committee of five, one of them Cardinal Rampolla, to discuss the matter thoroughly and report to him. Later he was to issue an opinion in the form of an encyclical letter, *Graves de communi re*. It appeared early in 1901, and was a clear and concise statement, a summing up briefly of *Rerum Novarum* and a further definition of some of its statements.

For economic and philosophic treatment *Rerum Novarum* would remain the document to consult. The minor matters which had since come up Leo handled as best he could in this second paper. He answered the objections to the name of the movement by saying he had not liked the term Social Democracy and Christian Democracy seemed acceptable. To those who said the term had the sense of implying a democracy that was a popular government, he wrote, "It really has no political reference. We meant a beneficent Christian action working for the people; the word Christian makes the phrase clearly one where the Christian faith, its morals and its disciplines, are paramount." It did not mean that one kind of government was better than another. It simply wanted working people to have the advantages so clearly theirs, and its basic aim was to bring back "those engaged in manual work to less difficult conditions." As such it was, he said, in full accord with both natural and divine law. Its chief implication was that all Christians must work together for the common good.

"None is so rich and powerful as to have no need of anyone, and no one is so poor that he cannot in some way help others," he wrote. He counseled unity of direction of clergy and laity to instill right principles, to show deference to authority, to do honest work, to make religion an essential part of life. And once again he insisted that the entire social problem was not merely economic, as Marx said, but that it was first of all moral and religious and its solution must be formal and religious. Then the world would see "a new and changed society, one which would count it an honor to bend the knee to God."

"Rome has spoken" was the jubilant shout of Christian Democrats when the second encyclical was published. Many accepted it in exactly the sense the pope had intended, but he learned that some, especially the younger workers, were putting their own interpretation on parts of it. So, through the pen of Cardinal Rampolla, a letter went out explaining that anyone could express political opinions but he must not speak in the name of the Church when doing so. In other words, it was a warning both to those who did not want to move at all and to those who wanted to move too fast, who were placing too much emphasis on the material good and too little on the spiritual. Both were important but one fact was clear above all the debates and must be kept so—all social classes, including the highest as well as the humblest, must be secure in a government which worked for the benefit of all.

Several years before, a bishop had written, after a visit to the Vatican: "The prisoner in the Vatican who, one would think, would be forced to remain aloof from the movements of the world is the man who seems best to know its aspirations and needs." *Rerum Novarum* and this second letter seemed to say amen to that remark.

Leo was to speak insistently before long to the French bishops: "Go to the people. Go to the workers. Go to the poor." Early in 1900 he spoke warningly and sadly, "The melancholy reality cries and cries aloud, that we have today great need of courage in working together."

He spoke with bitter truth. In 1894 President Carnot of France had been killed; four years later Elizabeth of Austria was killed. In 1900 King Humbert of Italy was assassinated and a year later, President McKinley. Stories of riots and strikes had come from both Europe and the United States. Was this a time, he asked, for Catholics to indulge in vain argument about the names of an organization or speak bitter denunciation or satiric blasts?

Soon after the issuance of the second encyclical came the pope's birthday and Cardinal Oreglia was chosen to give the congratulatory address of the cardinals. One of the most conservative in the Sacred College, he managed to slip in along with the congratulations a few lines showing his own disapproval of Christian Democracy.

The pope, who had seen the address before it was read aloud, replied only to the congratulatory part, and very courteously. The rest of it, he said even more courteously, would be answered next day in *Osservatore Romano*. When it was read, it proved to be only a further series of pleasant words about Christian Democracy.

Not long afterwards Leo heard that the young editors of *Il Domani d'Italia,* the organ of the Christian Democrats in Rome, were in financial troubles. They were in debt for some thousands of lire and when they asked the papal secretary of state for help, they were turned down. They thereupon wrote a spirited editorial about the refusal.

Leo, after hearing about the deficit, sent word that he would make it up. "But surely they should first apologize to the cardinal," someone remonstrated.

The pope smiled and shook his head. "If they had not taken so great an interest in their cause they would not have been so treated," he said.

Chapter Thirteen

THERE had over the years been considerable difficulty in Leo's relations with France, but he had never lost his affection for that country. He understood to some extent the intransigence of the conservative monarchical groups, even though he knew it did not make for better relations with the Vatican. The odd fact was that this group agreed in one thing with the radicals who were largely in control of the government—neither of these very disparate groups wanted any recognition by the Vatican of France as a republic.

Anarchists in Paris said amusedly that the French Catholics were more Catholic than the pope. In a way this was very true, for they felt that a return of the monarchy was the only way to save the Faith in France. They resented having the pope say there ought now to be an "acceptance of new governments established *de facto* in place of former governments which *de facto* were no more." The French Catholics, however, were angry at being denounced by statements like that "made by a very old man." They could not, or at least refused to, see that democracy could ever take the place of the old dynasties which had received the blessings of earlier popes or that democracy was now a living force.

Leo, who had been watching closely what was going on in France, saw the situation there more clearly than did the

French Catholics. The republic proclaimed there in 1870 was apparently going to continue. There was no evidence of a desire to return to a monarchy, at least not among the majority of the citizens. Then, too, he had to consider that the Vatican had a definite policy regarding the recognition of established governments.

In 1890 he had a long talk with Cardinal Lavigerie of Paris and told him the policy on which he had decided. "Perhaps it is time," he said, "that the closely closed window of the religious façade be opened." The cardinal had himself that same year in one of his talks to officers of the French Navy in Algiers, said, "Union is our great need. The time has come to declare the ordeal over, to end our dissonance and make a sacrifice for the sake of our country." Now he was happy to hear that the pope intended to act.

Leo's definite decision came in the form of an encyclical epistle in 1892 to the French people. In *Au milieu des solicitudes* he spoke of his affection for France, an affection he had held since he was a young man. He felt that the time had now come when there must be unity of Catholics in their country. He realized there was still legislative hostility to the Church and that he deplored, but he felt that the time had come to put away political dissonance: "The Catholics of France ought to unite to sustain their cause and in that way dissipate the prejudice of others." He wanted them to cease upholding the royalist cause and accept "the powers constituted and existing among you." "Governments change," he wrote, "and no one can consider any form of civil government as so definite that it must remain forever immutable."

This statement greatly irritated many of the monarchists who promptly cut their Peter's Pence collections and said that those who rallied to the pope's request were "kissing the republican foot of their executioners." Several French bishops came to Rome to argue the pope's statement. He listened quietly to their objections, as voiced by their constituents, and then said, "I want to commit the Church so deeply and fully that my successor cannot turn it back." And he added that he agreed with the statement of the cardinal of Paris, which they no doubt also knew, that the important thing was to look for agreements and turn from differences.

Gradually but slowly, the climate changed and cooled. As he said in his encyclical, there was a distinction between the form of government, which could be accepted, and the laws, which could always be amended. The form must be adapted to the nation.

When he gave an interview to a journalist who represented *Le Petit Journal* of Paris, he said he thought that now all Frenchmen, religious and lay, should unite on this matter: "The republic is as legitimate a form of government as any other," and he spoke of the United States. He had just seen representatives of the forthcoming Chicago Exposition who had arrived in Rome to invite the Vatican to participate and he had discussed their government with them.

"The United States with its republican form of government," he told the journalist, "and despite possible dangers from a liberty almost boundless, grows greater every day and the Catholic Church there has developed without any struggle against the state. What is suitable for the United States is also suitable—perhaps even more so—in republican France."

When a French bishop wrote an irritated letter to Cardinal Rampolla, that diplomatic prelate said that the Church was not against any form of government and that Catholics should not make the interests of the Church subordinate to the struggles of political parties—and added persuasively that he hoped they would understand and work with the Church.

During 1893 the four-hundredth anniversary of the discovery of America was celebrated. It was planned to make it a great occasion in the United States and Leo followed the preparations with deep interest. He had told the officials who came to ask him to take part that he would be happy to do so, and offered them papal properties for an exhibit. He said he would send Monsignor Satolli to be their custodian.

The summer before he had written an encyclical epistle—*Quarto abeunte saeculo*—addressed to the bishops of Spain, Italy and the two Americas, in which he noted there was a deep fitness in joining in the commemoration of Columbus' exploit—"for he is ours, too, if we give a little consideration to the particular reason for his plan for exploring the *mare tenebrosum*. It is certain that the Catholic faith was the strongest motive in the decision."

He spoke of the many difficulties Columbus had to meet—the adverse opinions of the learned, the rebuffs from those in high places, the disloyalty of some of his companions, the storms and long vigils at sea, the jealous calumny, the conspiracies—he had lived through them all and won. He had discovered America at a time when a great storm was about to break on the Church and it seemed as if he were designed by a special plan of God to compensate for the injury she was to suffer in Europe.

The Exposition in Chicago, in which at first some of the bishops had not wished to participate, proved to be a great and happy success. The pontifical exhibit sent by Leo was an exact reproduction of the convent at La Rabida; it held many books and manuscripts, letters and reports which the Vatican possessed relating to the discoveries of Columbus. The history of the little convent was told to interested visitors, and there were many. The story was that Columbus, disappointed in his efforts to raise funds for his exploration, left Granada and with his young son wandered about Spain, poor and shelterless. They found a refuge in the Franciscan convent of La Rabida where he told the prior of his efforts and their failure. The prior was confessor to Queen Isabella and through him the queen grew interested in the plans of Columbus and came to his help.

One feature of the exposition was the speech by Monsignor Satolli; another was the presence of Cardinal Gibbons. Two years later Leo established in the United States an apostolic delegation and chose Satolli, now archbishop, to head it—"hoping thus to draw more closely the bonds of duty and friendship with the United States." The pope wrote of the equity of laws in that country, of the freedom of the Church there—"free to live and act without a hindrance."

The pope's episcopal golden jubilee came in February of 1893 and the bells rang all over Rome to herald the occasion. The crowds who came to the Vatican were happy to see the pope looking so well. On the night of the jubilee the great basilica was brightly illuminated—for the first time since 1870.

Again the pilgrims came, bringing their gifts, some from as far away as Jerusalem. A letter arrived from the Shah of Persia, which began, "Most respected and honored." A few days later the German emperor and his wife came to pay their respects. Almost every country in Europe sent representatives—all, that is, save the Italian government. From it came no message at all.

Two years later took place a very different celebration in Rome—the twenty-fifth anniversary of the occupation of the city by national troops. In recognition of the date on which Rome became part of a united Italy, crowds gathered everywhere in the city to celebrate it, and they did so in noisy fashion. There was a huge military pageant and early in the evening a parade swept past the Vatican singing songs of a free Italy.

Leo was sitting in his garden when he heard the rough yells on the other side of the wall. It was very evident that no one was sparing his feelings in the slightest by keeping the demonstration at a distance. He listened and though his face grew white and his eyes blazed, he said nothing at all when he was taken back to his apartments. However, sheer indignation that even in his quiet prison he should be thus insulted, proved too much for him and he made a written protest to the Roman authorities.

"The sentiments of humanity," he wrote, "would seem to permit some consideration in our old age. It has been totally ignored. What pains Us is the intent to perpetuate rather than terminate a conflict, to pursue an essentially antireligious aim, to change the destinies of Rome, to make her again pagan. . . . noisy demonstrations led by a sect who are the enemies of God . . . nothing can confer true independence for the papacy as long as it has no temporal jurisdiction. . . . and only recently we have been confronted by veiled threats to abrogate even existing papal guarantees."

Though it was a dignified protest many thought it should not have been made. Other people, however, considered it a fine document and liked the way the old pope had answered a personal affront with honest anger.

In 1886 there had taken place the presentation of the cause of the English Martyrs, fifty in all. Two of them were so exemplary, Thomas More and Bishop Fisher, that Leo declared them blessed without the usual procedure.

Like France, England was dear to Leo. The matter of reunion with the Anglican church was one he regarded with real hope, for it represented peace and unity. He visioned a collective union which a recognition of Anglican orders might bring about.

This idea of reunion of sects which had broken away led him also to speak often of a *rapprochement* between the Western and the Eastern Church. In 1893 he had suggested a Eucharistic Congress be held in Jerusalem, an idea which at first caused consternation in various countries. However, on the promise that it would be nonpolitical and limit itself to the field of Christian piety, all breathed more easily and agreed. The Sultan promised to keep order in Jerusalem. The Russians agreed. Cardinal Langevieux was sent as papal delegate for the occasion. Greek and Latin patriarchs participated in one Mass. Each day the Mass was celebrated according to one of the Eastern rites of the churches who belonged to the Holy See. The dissident Eastern churches took no formal part in the congress but they met informally and talked together.

Six years after the beatification of More and Fisher, the pope received in audience Lord Halifax, president of the English Church Union, a high church Anglican group with a membership of thirty bishops and three thousand clergymen. The conversation turned to Halifax's favorite topic—some sort of reunion with the Holy See and the English Church. It was a delicate and difficult matter, as they both knew, but the earnestness and deep Christianity of the Englishman greatly moved the pope. From that time he considered the matter more carefully and from many angles. Not long after the visit of Halifax he received in audience the Princess of Wales, her two daughters and the Duke of York. His interest and his feeling of friendship deepened, until in 1895 he sent a message to England, entitled, "Leo XIII to the English people who seek the kingdom of Christ in the unity of faith." It was a long and affectionate epistle. It greatly impressed Gladstone among others, so much so that he wrote an article on the subject, in it a quotation from Coleridge:

> They parted ne'er to meet again,
> But neither ever found another
> To keep the hollow heart from pining.

Leo had spoken of the many English people who had come to see him in the past, of their hope that some day there would be unity of faith between them—"that great hope, the reunion of Christendom. We have therefore determined to write to all English who glory in the Christian name and invite them to this same work . . . to seek the help necessary for such a thing by prayer."

He spoke of the storms which had devastated Catholicism during the sixteenth century. As bishop of Perugia he had approved prayers for reunion when a member of an Anglican order, Father Ignatius Spencer, came to see him with a plan for a return of England to the Catholic Church. He spoke of the faith of England since the days of Gregory the Great. He spoke, too, of social problems and of how well England had handled the care of her aged and her orphans. He noted the strong sense of charity that she had never lost.

Leo spoke of the difficulties in the way of reunion which they all knew well: "Time has, of course, caused existing divisions to take deep root—but is that a reason to give up all hope of remedy?" He trusted that something would come out of all their hopes and their prayers and he prayed it might be soon—"for the time cannot be far distant when We render to God an account of our stewardship. How blessed it would be if We could bring Him the fruit of holy unity." He ended his letter by calling on as pleaders such saints as Gregory and Augustine and above all the Mother of God, for England had for centuries been known as the Dower of Mary.

The answer Archbishop Benson of Canterbury sent was an equally friendly though very diplomatic letter. He wrote that he was well aware of the pope's "transparent sincerity" and, as to one body in the future—"we too pray that we may be one in the oneness of the Father and the Son; that the peace of God shall rule over all our hearts at last . . . very steadfastly we pray this prayer." He had, he ended, recommended the matter to the prayers of the people of the Anglican Church.

During the next months various Anglican ministers who had become Catholics came to see the Holy Father. Terms on which Anglicans could be received into the Church were widely discussed. The matter became a burning issue and varying opinions were heard. Leo assured all his visitors of his hopes and said he knew that he and his successors would always be willing to sacrifice everything for this hope, with the exception of the sacred deposit of truth itself.

In a brief letter on Christmas Eve the pope wrote: "It would be the fullest realization of our vows if it should be given Us to hasten the arrival of the time promised by God when there will be one fold and one shepherd."

All through 1895 the discussions went on. Sometimes hope rose very high, sometimes it sank. But it was obvious to those most interested that difficulties were developing. A letter in June gave hints of trouble to come. For one thing, English Catholics had suffered too much in England in the fairly recent past to be eager to join their persecutors. Cardinal Vaughan went to Rome to explain to the pope that submission to the pope was an idea no bishop had even considered among the Anglican bishops. For the first time the pope understood the real difficulties in the way. "But then this is a question of doctrine," he said. Cardinal Vaughan said sadly that indeed it was.

Perhaps it was that so many people had been anxious that

some sort of unity become a fact that two things had been ignored. For one, no doubt some Catholics had fully expected the Anglicans to enter the Catholic Church in a body, while the Anglicans had thought of the word union not so much an integral union as merely an understanding. In the end, the fine effort failed. It failed not because of hopes and intentions but on purely legalistic grounds. It was, as the pope had said sadly, a question of doctrine.

In December the Vatican made public the decision. Anglican orders could not be recognized as valid. The review of the subject had been intensive and exhaustive. The committee appointed by Leo had searched out every fact. It was sad to read, after so many hopeful words, the statement that ordinations according to the Anglican rite "have been and are absolutely null and utterly void." A careful review of the history of the rite of Holy Orders set up under Edward VI showed that at that time the hierarchical succession had lapsed. And so the question of validity was closed.

Interestingly enough, the next year brought some fruits of Leo's endeavors, even though they were small. Several thousand schismatic Copts in Egypt returned to the Church and a bishop in Mesopotamia surrendered his orders and with his flock also returned.

Cries of "Americanism" had been heard for some years, in part in European cities, in part in the United States itself. It was very true that the more important figures in the Church in America at the time—Gibbons, Spaulding, Ireland among them—considered that the ideal for their country was a church American in language and manners. It was also clear they wanted no slightest relaxation of the ties which bound them to the Mother Church in Rome.

In 1895, due no doubt to the statements being made about

the Church in America, the pope sent an encyclical letter to the United States in which he reviewed its background from Columbus and the early missionaries. He also reviewed its progress in later years. He delineated the position and duties of the papal delegate whom he had sent there and spoke of the necessity for the observation of just civil laws, of the rights of the workers and the avoidance of secret societies. It was a general summary of the Church's stand in every country in the matter of discipline and principle, though it was applied in this case especially to the United States.

Archbishop Satolli was by now a part of the church scene in America. He had come first in 1893 to represent the Holy Father at the celebration of the first centenary of the hierarchy. The next year he had come as curator of the valuable collection sent to the Exposition. His talk there on the Gospel and the American Constitution had been well received.

When he was first appointed apostolic delegate to the United States, there were some in Rome who said openly that it was hoped he would keep an eye on Gibbons and Ireland and especially on Monsignor Keane, president of the Catholic University, under whom it had become a fine institution of advanced learning.

At first he disappointed those who desired that he would curb the prelates considered too liberal by the Old World group. He made no such effort. He became quite popular, even though some of the American clergy had viewed his appointment not exactly as an honor to them but rather as a sign that the Holy See did not trust them and had sent a watchman.

For a time all went well but the honeymoon did not last long. Satolli's first years had given him standing, mainly thanks to the efforts of Gibbons and Ireland in his behalf. But, as soon as he was established, he began to oppose them. Apparently what gave him his chance was the dissatisfaction of the head of dogmatic theology at the university, Dr. Schroeder, who had told his troubles to the papal delegate. Rumor said his distress was not primarily with academic matters but rather a resentment at Dr. Keane's support of Ireland in matters of education. He was aided in this by a small but vocal group at the university which murmured that Dr. Keane was departing from Catholic doctrine in his methods of instruction. Satolli sent word of this to Rome and he succeeded in 1896 in having Keane removed as president. The Vatican appointed in his place Monsignor Conaty and offered Monsignor Keane a post in Rome.

The American prelates were for the moment silent. However, when the new rector was being inducted into office, Cardinal Gibbons in his address praised not only the new head's fine qualities but also praised the former president— "the second founder of the Catholic University."

New criticism had come about with the publication of a biography of Isaac Hecker, founder of the Paulist Fathers, written by a member of his congregation. It had a foreword by Archbishop Ireland and a letter from Cardinal Gibbons. Had the book been more carefully read—and later more carefully translated into French—a clearer view of what was said in it might have been obtained. Abbé Klein had made not so much a literal translation as an adaptation. In the original the book showed clearly that the difficulties with which Hecker had met while he was still a Redemptorist were really part of a general debate among the various nationals in the United States—Irish, French and, in his special case, German. His chief plea had been that he and some of the American members of the congregation be allowed to preach in English instead of German in order to reach more people. No one had ever questioned his orthodoxy or the results of his preaching or that of the Congregation of St. Paul which Pius IX had given him permission to establish in the United States after the Redemptorist head in Rome had dismissed him.

On a visit to Rome several years before, Cardinal Gibbons had striven to reassure the pope that false conceptions of "Americanism" emanating from Europe simply had no foundation in reality. In fact, one bishop had been moved to remark that "as a heresy it exists only in the imagination of three or four Frenchmen." And it was very true that Leo himself had pointed out that the Church "has never neglected to adapt herself to the genius of nations." It was he who, when the Catholic University was first opened, insisted it have a distinctly American flavor and be conducted by American intellects. "If at first foreign talent is necessary, it must be with the view of later on developing home talents," he said.

However, the trouble which had started with the Hecker biography, and which had, to some extent, quieted down, was started again when in 1898 the biography was issued in a French version including the foreword by Archbishop Ireland.

There was a new papal delegate in Washington now and Satolli was back in Rome. Preparations were begun by the former delegate and his friends to have the French edition put on the Index. At almost the same time, in Paris, Abbé Maignen issued a pamphlet entitled *Is Father Hecker a Saint?* which was so phrased as to make Gibbons and Ireland look like rebellious priests. Cardinal Richard of Paris, made aware of this, refused to give it an imprimatur. It was, however, approved in Rome though later Cardinal Rampolla said, "The pope and I knew nothing about it at all." The French edition of Hecker's life was, however, never placed on the Index.

By that time the entire matter had grown to such proportions that the pope wrote an encyclical letter—*Testem bene-*

volentiae—on the subject of Americanism. He said that naturally he did not approve of innovations or false doctrines but that they must be proved to be so. He could not approve of what "in certain quarters is called Americanism. But if the word is used as signifying the constitution of your state and custom and laws, there is nothing in Americanism for Us to reject. And would not American bishops be the first to condemn it as an insult to themselves and the nation?"

The pope went on to say that the Church could always adapt herself to the exigencies of time and place. He said he was not unaware that in a country as new as the United States difficulties could develop regarding the Faith. But one of his conclusions was that much of the difficulty in this case was due to "abnormal views nurtured abroad," no doubt a diplomatic reference to the French objectors, for the encyclical especially took note, and by name, of the French translation of the Hecker book and the pope seemed to imply that something was perhaps also due to the poor translation.

Equally diplomatic, Cardinal Gibbons wrote, "All misunderstanding has been dispelled by the Holy See." He had been in Rome not too long before and expressed himself as amazed to find Leo so well despite his years and his heavy work. He was very pale and extremely thin, more bent than he had been on the prelate's previous visit a few years before, but his eyes were as bright, his voice as strong, his memory as phenomenal as ever, said the cardinal.

It was true that it was a joy to listen to the deep musical voice, to see the vitality of body and strength of mind of the old man who was now close to ninety years. He still walked very fast. "*Il papa corre sempre,*" said his attendants, shaking their heads but with pride in their voices. He still loved his garden and the small ceremony with which he went there every day by a definitely regulated regime. First he was carried out in the sedan chair to his carriage. After a short drive he got out and walked about, looking at his birds and his zoo, talking with the gardeners about the flowers and the condition of the grapes which produced wine he sent to friends.

It was true that he now, as a concession to his doctors, rose two hours later. He allowed himself a glass of champagne daily. But, except for the garden and a brief siesta, the day was filled with work, beginning after the early Masses and ending late at night. His delight when his official work was finished was to lose himself for a time in Dante or Horace or perhaps work for an hour at his own verses.

He had showed Cardinal Gibbons his most recent ode. It was on Frugality and Long Life and spoke first of a "spare board but with dishes bright and vintage pure" but the modest board did have on it "steaming bowls of Mocha to close the feast." And part one ended:

> If you diet thus then I'll engage
> You've found the secret of a green old age.

The second part described very fully a richly set table and then the sad results of gluttony.

Cardinal Gibbons reported to the United States Catholics that the pope had said to him, "The progress of religion in your country makes me rejoice. A republic where there is authority without despotism, belief without license and where the strength is in the people."

During the next year the pope suffered somewhat from arthritis. At the suggestion of several at the papal court, Father Kneipp, the famous Bavarian priest who had acquired a universal reputation for his cold-water therapy and who had a large institution in his native Germany, was invited to treat the pope. From the beginning many at the court had opposed it, feeling that the pope was too old for such a dras-

tic treatment as this of cold water. Eventually Father Kneipp
was sent home, but Leo, who had grown very fond of him,
though perhaps not of his method, consoled him by making
him a monsignor and having his picture taken with him, the
two sitting side by side.

Father Kneipp, however, was very sorry to have the treat-
ments stopped. "I could make him live to be a hundred if
those idiots had not stopped me," he said. "But as a matter of
fact His Holiness is very fortunate in that he really has no
body. When he took the baths I saw only a sort of specter.
Such a man cannot die like the others."

Just before the turn of the century a journalist had been
added to the small number fortunate enough to secure an interview with the pope. This time it was an American, James
Creelman. When he came to Rome and asked if it would be
possible to secure an interview, several cardinals shook their
heads. At last he learned that perhaps Cardinal Hohenlohe
could arrange it. The latter promised to try and two days later
Creelman was told the pope had agreed to see him. Monsignor Hooker, vice-rector at the American College, had
promised to act as interpreter.

The awed young man went with him to the Vatican, past
red-and-yellow-and-black-clad Swiss guards, up the marble
steps where at the top stood gendarmes of St. Peter's, to the
Hall of St. Clement where a knee-breeched servant took the
document admitting them. On again they went through room
after room to the throne room. Monsignor Hooker whispered
to Creelman that the workingmen of Rome had made the
throne as a gift for the pope. Above it was a triple crown
with azure shield, silver bar and pine tree, the coat of arms
of the Pecci family, the monsignor pointed out.

A chamberlain escorted them to a smaller room and there,

after all the pomp, after the complicated service, sat a gentle old man with sad dark eyes. He was all in white and wore a plain gold cross. He was so thin that the cross seemed sunk in him, thought Creelman.

He looked at his visitor and smiled. "You are very young," he said. "I had expected to see an older man—but then your nation, too, is young." And suddenly Creelman thought of two adjectives to apply to this man—majestic and appealing.

"I love the Americans," the pope went on. "I have a great tenderness for them all, Catholics and Protestant alike. There religion has liberty and so is a growing power for good. And besides they are so frank and unaffected. I sometimes feel I am more respected in America than in Europe. Here the power of paganism is at work and there is so much impending disorder—and yet only organized religion can restore moral balance to the human race."

The delighted Creelman—he had been told he might take a few notes as the monsignor translated—listened intently as the old man went on. "See what living without faith has brought people in this country—discontent, hatred, unhappiness. While I am still living I want to bring about a change in them. I want the employer and the worker to look at each other through Christian eyes. One cannot bring about contentment by legislation, but Christianity can bring them together in grace and peace and love. The trouble is that as wealth increases in the world the gulf will deepen unless Christian charity bridges it."

"Education perhaps, too, Your Holiness," ventured the American.

Leo nodded and then smiled suddenly as if aware that his visitor knew of his great passion for education. "Yes, that will do a great deal, for an enlightened man cannot be enslaved. That is why I worked to free slaves still held in Africa—you know about that?"

"Yes, I do, Your Holiness."

"I want to work until not one slave in the world is not free," said the pope energetically.

They turned to the subject of war and armies, and he looked very sad. "These vast armies, full of peril to souls, drawing away wealth needed elsewhere. The armies of Europe are impoverishing Europe, my son."

"In America our national policy is veering to arbitration rather than war," said Creelman.

Leo nodded. "That is a true and wise principle—and perhaps the only one. Oh, I would that those who govern Europe would be so guided, too."

There was deep affection in the old pope's face when he gave the eager young man his blessing and said good-by. Creelman looked back as he was leaving the room. In the shadows stood the slender white figure and the visitor went away feeling as if a spirit were watching him go.

Chapter Fourteen

ON Christmas Day of 1899 a Holy Year was begun with all the ancient ceremony. On that day Leo opened the Holy Door at St. Peter's, striking it with a gold mallet, and with great ceremony inaugurated a jubilee year of praise and prayer.

On New Year's Day the pope showed some of the cardinals an ode he had written on the opening day of the century, an Alcaic verse, Greek in form and filled with Horatian expression. It ended:

> Long ninety years my course has run—
> Thy will be done.
> My prayers, a crowning grace to gain,
> Be not in vain.

The celebrations during that Holy Year showed in what a high place he was held in the Catholic world. The pilgrims seemed to come in never-ending crowds. Some said Rome had never seen so many, that ten thousand came each week. They traveled from every land and they all wanted at least a glimpse of the Holy Father.

Although many groups were very large, there were small ones, too. One day the officers and crew of the American training ship *Dixie* were received in the Sistine Chapel. Seventy-five sailors stood before him waving the Stars and Stripes and then cheering him with loud American hurrahs.

One pilgrimage came from England led by the Duke of Norfolk. His message to Leo—and his gift—was the word that he had obtained the right to translate the relics of Saint Edmund, English king and martyr, from France. They were to be placed in the cathedral at Westminster.

Leo officiated to the year's end and his doctors admitted he seemed none the worse for his fatiguing months. They had asked him to skip some of the audiences but he refused. "Not when they have come so far," he said. "And look at me. I am enjoying it. I am very well." And they had to admit he was. "It is the excitement," he told them. "It is good for me."

People no longer spoke of his death but took his life for granted. Every day they saw him going about in the Vatican gardens, the limited area where he had for so many years found his small freedom. More than one newspaper commented on the fact that the Church, which a few years before had seemed on the point of reaching the nadir of its international importance, was entering now on an era of great vitality, that the papacy was more of a real force in the world at large than in the days of its temporal power. She had, as Leo phrased it, again regained her rhythm—"which once overcame and crushed paganism."

That could have been applied to him too. The old man whom all had expected to die soon after he came to the throne was still engaged in putting the past behind him as soon as it was no longer the present. He looked always at the future and what it had in store.

When, during the last year of Leo's life, Count von Bülow, the German chancellor, came to see him, he spoke afterward of his wonderful eyes: "They have in them the light of faith as the representative of Christ"—and then he added that they also held some of the "impalpable cynicism peculiar to Italian statesmen of the Holy See."

The latter statement was no doubt true. But what most people saw was chiefly the other-worldliness. "He seems to have taken over matter and so to speak absorbed it into himself," said one woman after an audience. "No taint of earth clings about him any more," wrote a reporter.

He had looked ready to leave the world when he was crowned almost twenty-five years before. He looked the same still—the features, a little thinner now, seeming to be carved from old ivory. He was a little more bent, but still quick in his movements. His voice was still clear and strong. When he came into view at an audience, someone said it was as if one of Fra Angelico's saints had stepped from a fresco on the wall and was lifting a hand in blessing.

When he talked with people it was always personal attention which he gave. The phrases were unhurried; the tone was intimate. His questions showed that he was listening closely. One pilgrim from the United States shook his head as he left the audience chamber. "What feeds the lamp in that frail vessel?" he asked in wonder.

Leo did not, despite his thinness, look at all cadaverous, old though he was. In fact, his silvery hair made him look no more than seventy. He still looked a great deal like the nuncio who sat next to Queen Victoria in Brussels in the 1840's. He still read a great deal. Lately the modern poets had interested him though he was critical of them. He still wanted news brought him the moment it arrived. He was still likely to be awake whatever the hour. He wrote less poetry but on Christmas night of 1901 he wrote a brief verse, gentle and appealing, on peace:

> Come, Christmas peace
> And nevermore depart.
> Link us together, hand in hand
> And heart to heart.

During 1902 he issued nine encyclical letters and epistles, more than during any year of his reign. One was a long review of his pontificate in which he went over everything of importance he had spoken for or against. In another he urged resistance to the evils of socialism and anarchism. He defined the nature of a Christian education. He called on the press to defend the Church. One letter was on missionary work in the United States, especially for the Indian and Negro, and he praised the generosity of American Catholics to the Holy See. Other letters were on a new Catholic university in Austria; on the Eucharist, urging all to frequent Communion; on the Church in the Philippines with careful directions for its future growth; on a commission of Biblical studies which urged the study of philosophy, of ancient and oriental languages, stating he had set aside a part of the Vatican library for such a commission.

One letter was addressed to Bohemia and Moravia, where conditions were bad, and he warned against violence. Another was on the better education of the clergy, that seminaries educate the mind as well as the heart, that candidates for the priesthood study documents and special questions and Christian democracy even though they abstained from external action. One expressed grief at the legislation on civil marriage and divorce, and then summarized once more the teaching of the Church on those matters.

The encyclicals were so comprehensive and covered so much that it seemed almost as if he were hurrying to repeat once more all he had been saying to his people during the last quarter of a century.

On March 2, 1903, Leo was ninety-three years old. On that day he received in his library forty-two cardinals, many of them come to help celebrate his silver anniversary as pope. The cardinal who had feared he would die a few weeks after his selection to the papacy was, after twenty-five years, still on the throne.

He listened to their graceful tribute and thanked them. Then he gave each of them a copy of a beautifully bound pamphlet which reviewed the chief results of his reign and gave each a copy of a Latin poem he had written for his birthday—"my latest—and my last," he told them. When they read it afterward they agreed it was almost an elegy:

> Leo, now sets thy sun. Pale in its dying ray
> Black night succeeds the day.
> Black night for thee. The flood of life sustains
> No more thy shrunken veins.
>
> But thy freed soul escapes her chains and longs in flight
> To reach the realms of light.
> That is the goal she seeks; thither her journey fares.
> Grant, Lord, my anxious prayers.
>
> And may I see her face, Heaven's Queen, whose love each day
> Has brought me through the perils of the way—
> To her I lift my lay.

The next day marked the beginning of the anniversary of his silver jubilee as pope. "I never expected to see this day," he said that morning.

It was made a very great occasion. By eight in the morning the plaza at St. Peter's was jammed with eighty thousand people. Fifty thousand of them were admitted to the basilica for the High Mass of Thanksgiving.

During the celebration Leo took an active part in the various receptions and he gave many audiences. But that year for the first time people mentioned his increasing pallor and said his voice was noticeably weaker than in other years. But his delight in people was unimpaired and he still enjoyed meeting them. He still seemed better rather than weary from such efforts.

At one of the audiences there were introduced to him three young women, students from the College of the Sacred Heart in Boston. When they came to kneel for his blessing, the monsignor beside him explained who they were and he talked with them gaily in French.

"And what pleased you most in Rome?" he asked.

"This audience with Your Holiness," said one girl promptly.

He smiled at her teasingly. "Ah, you are flattering me—and here I had thought the Americans a truth-telling people!"

When they left the three looked back from the doorway and the old man and the girls smiled again at each other. "See," he said to those about him, "my American children really love me."

Those close to him realized that he was failing rapidly and no doubt he realized it himself, but he continued his usual life. There were still visitors even though the audiences were now, by order of his doctors, curtailed.

King Edward of England came in April, Emperor Wilhelm of Germany in May. One of the last to come to him in audience was a Passionist priest from the United States who brought a beautifully bound volume of the messages of the presidents. Leo talked also with a group of French cardinals about conditions in their country. He discussed matters of state with Rampolla and others.

He still liked to stay up very late, but early in July, when he came in from the gardens, he was very tired and went to bed immediately. There had been two consistories that month and no doubt they had taken a toll of his waning strength. Next day he was still not well but he refused to stay in bed. Instead he sat in a chair for the day and stayed in it until very late at night, almost as if he feared he would never leave the bed again if he gave in and retired. The doctors who came to examine him feared he had incipient pneumonia, a serious thing in so old a man. They insisted he go to bed and stay there. This time he was willing. He was very tired.

Cardinals came into the room for his blessing and to kiss his ring. Each time he tried to sit up and say a few words of courtesy but the effort soon proved too much. His nephews came and he smiled when he saw them. They were all that was left of the once-large family. He had outlived all the rest.

The frail body still pushed death away. To the astonishment of all he grew better as the days went on. He seemed actually to be convalescing. As Cardinal Manning said, he was a man who dearly loved life and looked on his own long one as a grace from Heaven.

In the first week of July he felt so much better that he began to work on verses he had been planning for St. Anselm's feast. He asked Rampolla for news from abroad and at home. Suddenly, while his secretary of state stood by his bed, he said, "I have been wondering how people will judge me after I am gone. But this I know—that I have always and greatly loved the Church and tried to work for her good and win it for her. So I can die tranquil."

When his doctor came in later he found him happily reading Horace's *Ars Poetica*. But later that day, and for the first time, it was noted that the clear mind was wandering, even though only occasionally. A few days later, when a group of cardinals stood about his bed, he smiled at them reassuringly. "I love you all," he said, and then he sighed, "but I am very tired and glad to go."

On July 19 it was clear that the end was near. St. Peter's plaza was crowded with people staring intently at the pope's windows. In every church the Blessed Sacrament was exposed. All over the world people were praying for him.

Next morning he was in a coma from which it was feared he would not emerge. But in the afternoon he suddenly opened his eyes, lifted a weak hand to the cardinals kneeling about his bed and said in a strong voice, "Be this my last blessing." A moment later he was dead. He was just four months past his ninety-third birthday.

When word went through the Vatican that he was gone, the people all through the palace wept, from cardinals to gardeners. When word went out to the crowds in the plaza, the sounds of weeping were plain.

The news sped to the world. When one paper said that no man's death had ever produced so wide a sensation, it was not far from the truth. The flags in every large city in the civilized world were at half mast. Messages of sympathy came to the Vatican from men and women of every creed, from Mohammedans as well as from Protestants and Catholics.

The Vatican gates were closed. The Franciscan Conventuals gathered about the pope's bed to pray. The Fisherman's Ring was taken from his finger and broken, according to the custom. He was arrayed in his vestments—the pallium over his shoulders, his ivory cross on his breast, a mitre on his head. With an escort of cardinals and court officials, he was taken to the throne room and placed under a canopy.

Next day, clothed in pontifical vestments of white and red, the body was taken to St. Peter's by the men who had always carried him on his sedia. Others preceded them holding lighted candles. Six bells, tolled only for the passing of a pope, were ringing. When the bier reached the altar of St. Peter, it was placed there and cardinals and Noble Guards formed a semicircle around the body while the Libera Me was chanted. Then Cardinal Rampolla, as archpriest of St. Peter's, gave the absolution and said the last prayers. The bier was lifted and the procession went on to the Chapel of the Blessed Sacrament where the body was to repose until Saturday.

Great throngs came to look at him and pray for him, gazing through the closed rail in front of the chapel. Tall candles stood about the bier. The immovable Noble Guard stood watch.

This was a very different burial from that of Pius IX. At that time St. Peter's had been closed all day and at night the cardinals had assembled in the Vatican with the clergy, gathered for what was really a secret ceremony.

Now crowds came and went. Some said that half of Rome had passed the pope's body. One feature made it very different from the earlier papal death—the presence of several groups of Italian soldiers stationed in the basilica to guard the great church and to keep order among the crowds. It was a small thing perhaps and not noted by many in the great mass of people. But the Vatican had taken keen note of it. "It is an unexpected tribute," said Cardinal Oreglia, "which no one could ever have imagined twenty-five years ago." He could speak with authority, for he was the only cardinal left alive not created by Leo and the only one to outlive him. To him the Italian government's gesture was not small but very large indeed.

On Saturday, July 25, the great doors of St. Peter's were closed. That evening the interment took place, with cardinals and diplomatic corps and specially invited guests in attendance, some two thousand in all. The body was carried from the chapel by clergy of the cathedral, to the sound of the choir singing the Miserere.

Everywhere was purple and black, the papal mourning

colors. Three coffins, one of lead and two of wood, rested on the Gospel side of the altar. The corpse was blessed for the last time and then lowered into the cypress coffin. The pope's face was covered with a white silk cloth and a red veil was placed over the entire body. Two documents were read, one a brief biography of the dead man, the other a burial record. At the foot of the body were placed three bags of gold, silver and bronze medals, all struck off during his lifetime.

Then the coffin was closed and sealed with six seals. Over it were placed two wide bands of violet velvet like a cross. On the lead coffin were placed the same number of seals and on this was also placed a death's head with crossbones and beneath it the place of the pope's birth, the date, the length of his reign and the date of his death. Then the cover of the third coffin was screwed down. With the choir singing the Benedictus, the cardinals went with the body to the temporary place of burial in the Vatican.

Next morning the people who came there saw the tomb closed and sealed, the triple crown over it but without the keys, and in gold letters, "Leo XIII. Pont. Max."

In another corner of the great basilica was an ancient tomb on which were words that would have fitted well Leo's own life: "He lived in virtue, he lives in the memory, he will live in glory."

He would live not only for his words, his holy life, but for the material things he had accomplished. When he died the Church in Germany was free and strong, the head of the government his friend. The English king had broken precedent by coming to visit him. Relations between the Holy See and Russia were cordial. Swiss Catholics had recovered their rights to education. Spain and Belgium and Austria had cause to be grateful to the pope. As for the United States, Leo himself phrased the sentiments of that young

land some years before, echoing a similar statement by
Gregory XVI: "Nowhere am I more truly pope than in the
United States."

Of thousands of tributes in newspapers and magazines to
Leo XIII perhaps the brilliant French writer Brunetière said
it best: "Catholic action has been oriented for long years,
perhaps for centuries, in the direction given by the great
pope who has gone. It will be the eternal glory of Pope Leo
XIII in history that he understood it."

Among the many Protestant tributes was one from an
American minister. In a sermon preached in his Presby-
terian church Dr. Mendenhall said, "Differ we may, but
one thing makes us one. We are children of one common
Father—and we were one in church life, all one, years ago.
Who knows but we may because of Leo XIII see with clearer
vision in the coming years."

BIBLIOGRAPHY

Begni, Ernesto (ed.). *The Vatican: Its History, Its Treasures.* New York: Letters and Arts Publishing Co., 1914.

Clarke, Richard H. *The Life of His Holiness, Pope Leo XIII.* Philadelphia: P. W. Ziegler and Co., 1903.

Claudia, Sister M., I.H.M. (comp.). *Dictionary of Papal Pronouncements: Leo XIII to Pius XII (1878 to 1957).* New York: P. J. Kenedy, 1958.

Creelman, James. *On the Great Highway.* Boston: Lothrop Publishing Co., 1901.

de Narfon, Julien. *Pope Leo XIII, His Life and His Work.* London: Chapman and Hall, 1899.

Descostes, François. *La Jeunesse de Léon XIII.* Paris: de Soye et Fils.

Fülöp-Miller, René. *Leo XIII and Our Times.* Translated by Conrad Bonacine. Toronto: Longmans, Green and Co., 1937.

Gilson, Étienne. *The Church Speaks to the Modern World: Social Teachings of Leo XIII.* Image Books.

Graham, Robert A., S.J. *Vatican Diplomacy.* Princeton: Princeton University Press, 1959.

Hales, E. E. Y. *The Catholic Church in the Modern World.* New York: Hanover House, 1958.

Hall, A. D. *A Life of the Pope: Leo XIII.* New York: Street and Smith, 1899.

McCarthy, Justin. *Pope Leo XIII.* New York: Frederick Warne and Co., 1897.

Pecci, Cardinal. *Pastoral Letter for Lent of 1887: Church and Civilization.* M. H. Gill and Son, 1888.

Pichon, Charles. *The Vatican and Its Role in World Affairs.* New York: E. P. Dutton and Co., Inc., 1950.

Seldes, George. *The Vatican: Yesterday, Today, Tomorrow.* New York: Harper and Brothers, 1934.

Soderini, Eduardo. *Pope Leo XIII.* Translated by Barbara Carter. Vol. 1. London: Burns, Oates and Washbourne, Ltd., 1934.

Talbot, James F. *Pope Leo XIII.* Boston: Martin Garrison and Co., 1885.

von Bilger, D. H. *Die Pecci in Carpineto.* Schwerin: L. Dipple.

Will, Allen Sinclair. *Life of Cardinal Gibbons.* New York: E. P. Dutton and Co., Inc., 1922.

Williams, Michael. *The Shadow of the Pope.* New York: Whittlesey House, 1932.

After Forty Years, encyclical of Pius XI on Labor and Capital. *N.Y. Times,* May 24, 1931.

The Latin Poems of Leo XIII. Translated by the Jesuits of Woodstock College. Baltimore: Hill and Harvey, 1887.

Life of Pius X. New York: Benziger Brothers, Inc., 1904.

Poems and Charades and Inscriptions by Leo XIII. Translated into English by H. T. Henry. New York: Dolphin Press, American Catholic Review, 1902.

Catholic Digest, *passim.*

Catholic Encyclopedia, *passim.*

Encyclopaedia Britannica, *passim.*

Index